Other Middle-Grade Books by Michael P. Spradlin

THE WWII ADVENTURES
Into the Killing Seas
The Enemy Above
Prisoner of War

THE KILLER SPECIES SERIES
Killer Species
Feeding Frenzy
Out for Blood
Ultimate Attack

THE YOUNGEST TEMPLAR SERIES
Keeper of the Grail
Trail of Fate
Orphan of Destiny

MEDAL OF HONOR SERIES
Jack Montgomery: World War II: Gallantry at Anzio
Ryan Pitts: Afghanistan: A Firefight in the Mountains of Wanat
Leo Thorsness: Vietnam: Valor in the Sky

PARARESCUE SERIES
Denali Storm

MICHAEL P. SPRADLIN

CLOSE CALLS

HOW ELEVEN US PRESIDENTS ESCAPED FROM THE BRINK OF DEATH

BLOOMSBURY
CHILDREN'S BOOKS
NEW YORK LONDON OXFORD NEW DELHI SYDNEY

BLOOMSBURY CHILDREN'S BOOKS
Bloomsbury Publishing Inc., part of Bloomsbury Publishing Plc
1385 Broadway, New York, NY 10018

BLOOMSBURY, BLOOMSBURY CHILDREN'S BOOKS, and the Diana logo
are trademarks of Bloomsbury Publishing Plc

First published in the United States of America in January 2020
by Bloomsbury Children's Books

Bloomsbury Publishing Plc does not have any control over, or responsibility for, any third-party websites
referred to or in this book. All internet addresses given in this book were correct at the time of going to press.
The author and publisher regret any inconvenience caused if addresses have changed or sites have ceased to
exist, but can accept no responsibility for any such changes.

Bloomsbury books may be purchased for business or promotional use. For information on bulk purchases
please contact Macmillan Corporate and Premium Sales Department at
specialmarkets@macmillan.com

Library of Congress Cataloging-in-Publication Data
Names: Spradlin, Michael P., author.
Title: Close calls : how eleven US Presidents escaped from the brink of death / Michael Spradlin.
Other titles: How eleven US Presidents escaped from the brink of death
Description: New York : Bloomsbury, 2020.
Summary: Historians tell the stories of tragic and untimely presidential deaths, but often
forgotten are the near misses. JFK and his fellow servicemen spent six days on a desert island
with only coconuts to eat after a deadly attack during WWII. Abe Lincoln was forced to take a
train trip in disguise, while America's first female detective worked to foil an early assassination
attempt. And when Andrew Jackson was attacked by an upset citizen who had been stalking
him for months, frontiersman Davy Crockett was the one to save him. With pacy, immediate
writing, this book chronicles thrilling, undertold stories of US presidents' moments of bravery.
Identifiers: LCCN 2019019164 (print) | LCCN 2019980875 (e-book)
ISBN 978-1-5476-0023-6 (hardcover) • ISBN 978-1-5476-0139-4 (e-book)
Subjects: LCSH: Presidents—United States—Biography—Miscellanea—Juvenile literature. |
Presidents—United States—Miscellanea—Juvenile literature. | Presidents—Assassination
attempts—United States—History—Juvenile literature. | Near-death experiences—
United States—Juvenile literature.
Classification: LCC E176.1.S6974 2020 (print) | LCC E176.1 (e-book) | DDC 973.09/9 [B]—dc23
LC record available at https://lccn.loc.gov/2019019164
LC e-book record available at https://lccn.loc.gov/2019980875

Book design by John Candell
Typeset by Westchester Publishing Services
Printed and bound in the U.S.A. by Berryville Graphics Inc., Berryville, Virginia
2 4 6 8 10 9 7 5 3 1

All papers used by Bloomsbury Publishing Plc are natural, recyclable products made
from wood grown in well-managed forests. The manufacturing processes conform to
the environmental regulations of the country of origin.

To find out more about our authors and books visit www.bloomsbury.com
and sign up for our newsletters.

"To be good, and to do good, is all we have to do."
—John Adams

CONTENTS

INTRODUCTION IX

1. IF THEY KILL THE GENERAL, HE CAN'T BE
   THE FATHER OF HIS COUNTRY 1

2. BEATING THE ODDS 13

3. THE BALTIMORE PLOT 21

4. FIRST YOU GET SHOT, THEN YOU GIVE A SPEECH 35

5. A SHOOTOUT WITH THE CAPITOL POLICE 43

6. I DON'T LIKE IKE 51

7. PT–109 59

8. THE FALL OF GERALD FORD 71

9. IN THE BELLY OF THE BEAST 79

10. "HONEY, I FORGOT TO DUCK!" 85

11. A YOUNG PILOT SAVED FROM CAPTURE 95

SOURCES 104

INDEX 111

INTRODUCTION

TODAY THE PRESIDENT OF the United States is often referred to as the most powerful person in the world. But it wasn't always that way.

In the early days of the republic, the president was often not the most powerful person in the room, let alone the world. The United States was a young country—with a new constitution, government, and system of laws—figuring things out as it went along. America was rich in resources, but the nation struggled to build an economy and infrastructure that could support its developing society.

Then, as now, becoming the president of the United States required several distinct personality traits. A potential president still has to be ambitious, able to communicate ideas, and unwilling to accept defeat easily. These are among the same characteristics that allowed many of our past presidents to stare death in the face—and survive!

Some of our presidents were tested in the crucible of wartime service before they ever made it to the Oval Office. Commanders in chief who were also war veterans started with General Washington, who bore the pressure of trying to defeat the greatest military power in the world, and continued to President George H. W. Bush, who became one of the youngest navy pilots in World War II. These people answered their nation's call, and in doing so, dramatically increased their own chances of having a close call. Luckily, these future presidents survived their wartime near misses. Other presidents would narrowly escape death and injury while in office—like Andrew Jackson, the first president to survive an assassination attempt.

All of the presidents in this book had the determination, drive, and, yes, luck to survive life-threatening odds.

The world has changed since those early days of the republic, and the dangers today may be different from those in history. But one thing future presidents will have is knowledge of how their predecessors survived their close encounters of the near-deadly kind.

IF THEY KILL THE GENERAL, HE CAN'T BE THE FATHER OF HIS COUNTRY

WHEN THE UNITED STATES declared its independence from Great Britain in 1776, King George III and his countrymen were pretty upset. Miffed. Angry actually.

They thought the American colonists should be grateful that they were being oppressed by the most powerful country in the world at the time. Sure, the colonists had to pay high taxes and fees. They didn't have a voice in their own parliament. They had to put up with British soldiers sleeping in their homes. If a colonist was charged with a crime, the crown was really fussy about granting a speedy trial. But other than these few minor inconveniences, many British felt the colonists should have been happy that they had Great Britain watching out for them. The British army and navy protected the colonies from attacks by other nations. And Britain was a market for crops and goods. So when

King George finally received a signed copy of the Declaration of Independence, he had a fit.

The first thing the king did was put a price on the head of every man who signed the Declaration. He also assumed his army and navy would pummel the colonies into submission in no time. But, was he ever wrong. The British military did beat up on the colonies, especially early in the war. But the colonials kept hanging on. They didn't fight fair. They didn't line up in neat rows on the battlefield, where every man could then be gunned down easily. Instead, they hid behind rocks and trees and launched ambushes. They fought in all kinds of ungentle-manly ways.

King George was especially peeved at General George Washington, who commanded the Continental Army. The guy just didn't know when he was beat. Eventually, it got to the point where several of the officers in the British army came up with a plan: kidnap and kill George Washington. It was a "cut off the head of the snake" type of approach. They figured that without Washington the rebellion would die. So, they set out to do it—twice.

The first attempt is sometimes referred to as the "Hickey plot," which was centered around a soldier named Thomas Hickey. He had become disillusioned with the rebel army and thought offing Washington might win him favor with the crown.

There are a few different versions of Hickey's plans. Hickey supposedly had the idea to sneak in some poisoned peas to the Washington household for the general to eat. Since peas were Washington's favorite veggie, this was probably a pretty sound plan.

In one telling, a tavernkeeper's daughter became friendly with

Hickey and learned of his plot. She was also a friend of General Washington through her father. She went to inform Washington of the plan right about dinnertime. He was about to take a bite of peas, and she snatched them out of his hands and dumped them out the window. According to the legend, some chickens outside scarfed down the peas and immediately keeled over dead. This is probably unlikely—although it makes a really good story, especially the keeling-over chickens part. What is far more likely is that Hickey was a blabbermouth when he was serving a prison sentence for passing counterfeit money. While in jail, he probably spilled the beans of the pea plan to another prisoner, who then tried to get out of jail faster by snitching on Hickey.

Either way, there really was a plot to assassinate Washington, and Hickey was a part of it. When the deadly dinner was exposed, it became clear that the plans went beyond just poisoned peas: it was a complicated plot, involving dozens of British operatives and soldiers. If the ruse had been successful, it most likely would have ended the revolution almost before it began. One American patriot described the derailed murder this way: "The greatest and vilest attempt ever made against our country; I mean the *plot*, the infernal *plot* which has been contrived by our enemies."

★ ★ ★

Washington purposely chose New York City as his base of operations for a variety of reasons. His headquarters on the island of Manhattan was accessible by water, which made a retreat possible by ship or boat if the redcoats took control of the King's Bridge, the span that connected northern Manhattan to the mainland.

The population of New York City in 1776 was around 25,000 people. It was the largest city located between Philadelphia and Boston, which allowed easier travel to important Revolutionary War battle sites. But the city was also a Tory (loyalist) stronghold, which made it a good place for a plot to assassinate General Washington to develop. All of the loyalists in New York made for a ready British spy network.

Washington was an observant fellow. After he arrived in New York to establish his headquarters, he realized that many Tories were feeding information to the British with no concerns about any consequences. So Washington decided that fear of reprisal was needed. He wrote a letter to the local Committee of Safety, telling them to "prevent any future correspondence with the enemy" and "to bring condign punishment [punishment that is deserved] [to] such Persons as may be hardy and wicked enough to carry it on."

But the committee dragged their feet for a few months, not really doing much at all to slow down the intelligence flowing to the British. So, when the British decided to come up with a plan to kill General Washington, there was little about his movements and habits they didn't know.

The principal leader of the British spy network was the loyalist Governor Tryon. The British were attempting a naval blockade of New York City, and Tryon sat in New York Harbor on a British warship.

The constant spying drove Washington batty. (Though of course he was running his own spy network, because, you know, war.) He wrote a letter to the Continental Congress: "The encouragements given by Governor Tryon to the disaffected,

THE HISTORY OF TORIES

After nearly 250 years, the story of the American Revolution has taken on a near-mythical status in American history. Today, the rebellion is viewed as a group of ragtag colonists, united in purpose: fighting against the most powerful nation in the world at the time. Every American was determined to end British rule.

This was not the case.

Opinion in the colonies was divided over the decision to declare independence from Great Britain. Many did not want to separate at all. Their businesses and livelihoods depended on the British markets. They required the British Navy to make sure their exports were safe and secure. Those who wished to remain loyal to Great Britain were called Tories or loyalists. Those who wanted to declare independence were called patriots or rebels.

Tories were just as adamant in their feelings as patriots. Many of the former kept their association with the king, offering financial support and assets to the crown. Many did so at great risk. Loyalists were disliked by patriots for their support of Great Britain. Some were imprisoned or had their property confiscated or destroyed. When the war began, some loyalists even went so far as

to return to England, even if they had been born in the colonies.

Tories acted as spies as well. In New York City, there were many loyalists who kept an eye on the comings and goings of the Continental Army and passed the information on to the British military.

which are circulated no one can tell how; the movements of this kind of people, which are more easy to perceive than describe." Meaning Governor Tryon was ticking him off.

Nobody seemed to be trying to help Washington ferret out the spies. He was a busy man. He knew he was going to have to fight the British somewhere around New York, and he was focused on that. Finally, the Committee of Safety reported to Washington that they had found . . . something. It was "a plot as has seldom appeared in the world since the fall of Adam," a "most dark and dreadful scheme to overthrow this once happy land." And the Tories? They "have a set time (when, we cannot find) to rise against the country." At last, someone other than Washington realized that people were out to get him.

It got worse. Not only were the loyalists spying and generally planning mischief in New York City, they were actually raising battalions of troops. They planned to train in secret and strike American positions to create chaos when the British regulars attacked. Poor General Washington had his hands full. Run a revolution, fight a war, try to stay alive. He was swamped.

It was at this point Washington learned that the main conspirators in the plot to kidnap and/or murder him had infiltrated his personal guard. And more to the point, Thomas Hickey, a member of that trusted guard, was involved in the plot up to his powdered wig. Washington had no tolerance for traitors. He decided there was a way to use Hickey to send a message to the loyalists in New York City that deceit would not be tolerated. And there was a good way to use Hickey for that purpose.

He would be hanged.

★　★　★

A second plot arose a few years later. This attempt on Washington's life was thwarted by an immigrant Irish tailor named Hercules Mulligan and his slave, Cato. Washington was saved because a British officer with loose lips needed a warm coat, and because Cato was willing to undertake an incredibly dangerous mission to save the general.

Hercules Mulligan landed in New York City when he was six years old. He learned the trade of a tailor and opened a shop in the city after attending King's College (renamed Columbia University after the Revolution). Mulligan was what is now commonly referred to as "a talker." A friendly, gregarious man, he could easily engage in conversation with a wide variety of people. His tailor shop served a large segment of upscale clientele, from New York City socialites to British Army and Navy officers. Mulligan was such a forceful and passionate speaker that he actually recruited Alexander Hamilton to the Sons of Liberty, a secret society composed of people who would become many of history's best-known patriots. Hamilton was seventeen years younger than Mulligan, an orphan, and flat broke when they met.

Like most colonists, Mulligan chafed at a British rule that grew more oppressive by the day. He was one of the first to join the Sons of Liberty. His tailor shop and the fact that he married a British admiral's niece put him a position to learn and hear a great deal about what the British were up to.

When his friend Alexander Hamilton attended King's College, he moved in with Mulligan, taking a room in his home. Hamilton was a studious, conscientious young man. Before long, he grew influenced by Mulligan's rising hatred of the British. Eventually Hamilton began writing essays and opinion pieces, which would lead him to a prominent role in writing *The Federalist Papers* after the war was won.

While Mulligan was busy clothing New York's elite in the latest fashions, the city continued to be a nest of spies. No one could be certain who was a loyalist or who was a patriot. One wrong word to the wrong person could send you to jail . . . or worse. To keep himself out of the clink, Hercules Mulligan learned to be very careful about speaking politics with any British clients or army officers.

Mulligan soon had the British believing he was loyal to the king. And it was this belief, that he was a loyalist, that brought him knowledge of a plot to kill Washington. One night, a British officer entered the tailor shop and insisted he needed a warm coat to cut the winter chill, and he needed it right away. Mulligan sensed something was up. But he acted casual, asking the officer why such a rush? The officer couldn't help talking about the plot. Mulligan wrote that he actually said, "Before another day, we'll have the rebel general in our hands."

When the British invaded and took over New York City, Mulligan tried to flee. He was not alone. Hundreds, if not thousands, of patriots raced out of the city. He was detained, but the British realized they needed to get their clothes somewhere, so Mulligan was let go, and he returned to his trade. Realizing that his shop was the perfect spot for gathering information and finding the British more and more annoying with each passing day, Mulligan began spying for the patriots.

While he was detained by the British, Mulligan met a man named Haym Salomon. Salomon was a Jewish immigrant from Poland who was fluent in several languages, which made him a valuable source of information. He also belonged to the Sons of Liberty. When he was captured, the British gave him a pardon but kept him aboard a British warship to translate for the Hessian troops the British had hired from Germany to fight against the Continental Army.

After Mulligan was released, he began sending advertisements for his shop to Salomon to be translated into German. Mulligan would make clothes for the Hessian officers. His slave, Cato, carried the ads to Salomon's office. He returned with intelligence that Salomon had gathered from his sources. Mulligan then passed the information along to his network of spies, where it would eventually reach General Washington's staff.

Cato became a valuable operative in Mulligan's spy network. At one point, Mulligan learned that the British would move south from New York in the summer of 1777, to try to take the colonial capital, Philadelphia. At first, the British didn't look at Cato as a messenger or a spy. When Mulligan sent the information about the troop movements, Cato was able to cross the Hudson River without a second look. The British paid no mind to a slave whom many of their officers were familiar with. Cato was able to deliver the information to Alexander Hamilton, now Washington's aide, without incident. The British general William Howe moved on Philadelphia, but Washington had set up defenses to slow any advance.

Mulligan and Cato persisted in aiding the patriots, despite at least two interrogations by wary British officers. Mulligan continued to collaborate with Haym Salomon, and he also teamed up with the New York–based patriot spy group called the Culper Ring.

In 1781, two years after Mulligan and Cato's Washington save, the import-export firm where Hercules's brother, Hugh, worked received a big rush order. Hugh learned that a troop of British cavalry was planning to capture General Washington in New London, Connecticut. Hercules Mulligan got the information to Alexander Hamilton, and Washington dodged the British again.

When the revolutionaries won the war, Mulligan, who looked like all the other wealthy New York loyalists, feared tarring and feathering or some other act of patriotic revenge. After all, he had been seen outfitting British officers almost daily. It would be easy for patriots to consider him a collaborator with the enemy. But George Washington remembered his "confidential correspondent." After the victory parade at the end of the war, as the procession marched through the streets of New York, Washington stopped at Mulligan's shop. He enjoyed breakfast with Mulligan, sending a message to everyone that the tailor was firmly in the patriot camp.

After the war ended, Mulligan proudly displayed a sign in his shop window. It read: Clothier to Gen'l Washington.

2

BEATING THE ODDS

JANUARY 30, 1835.

Angry politicians.

An angry electorate.

Conspiracy theories.

Elections that had been tampered with.

This is not a story about the twenty-first-century political climate in the United States.

Angry politicians, electorates, and conspiracy theories have been around since the dawn of democracy. And during the presidency of Andrew Jackson the anger was in full bloom. Jackson was a combative, divisive figure. He was blunt and abrupt in his dealings with both allies and enemies. And he was convinced those enemies had it in for him and were "out to get him."

Even if it meant ending his life.

CONGRESSMAN DAVID CROCKETT— KING OF THE WILD CONGRESS

They started out as friends but became political rivals.

In 1835 Congressman David "Davy" Crockett was one of the most famous people in America. His exploits as a soldier and frontiersman were the subject of biographies and stage plays. He was known far and wide as "the King of the Wild Frontier." And he used his fame to get himself elected to the US Congress.

Crockett was originally a "Jacksonian," a follower of President Andrew Jackson. Andrew Jackson was a powerful politician, especially in Crockett's native Tennessee. Crockett had already served terms in the Tennessee legislature before he was elected to Congress. His political career was started and fostered by his close relationship with Jackson. His reputation as a frontier fighter and woodsman gave him a reputation that served him well in office.

But the famous Crockett fell out of favor with Jackson. He opposed some of Jackson's policies, including the Indian Removal Act, which sent Native Americans from the southeast to reservations in Oklahoma territory west of the Mississippi River. Crockett disapproved of Jackson's plan for dealing with the tribes. Opposing other Jackson policies soon earned him Jackson's anger.

However, he interceded on the day an assassin tried to take Jackson's life.

When Crockett was voted out of office, he became discouraged with politics and wanted to make a new start. Crockett left for the Texas frontier, arriving in early 1836. He joined the Texas army and went to San Antonio, where he joined with the volunteers at the Alamo. When the Mexican army besieged and attacked the Alamo, Crockett died with the rest of the other defenders.

His death was mourned all over the country. Some even refused to believe he had been killed in the fighting. For years rumors of his continued existence cropped up around the country. In death, the legend of Davy Crockett only grew.

Andrew Jackson was the first sitting American president to experience an assassination attempt. A man name Richard Lawrence was the prospective assassin. President Jackson had been attending the funeral of South Carolina representative Warren Davis, held in the House Chamber of the Capitol. As the president exited the building, Lawrence approached him, removing a pistol from his cloak. He pulled the trigger and the percussion cap fired, but the powder did not ignite. It may have been that the damp weather ruined the gunpowder.

Regardless of the reason for the misfire, Lawrence pulled another pistol from his cloak. Incredibly, this one also did not fire correctly. President Jackson immediately realized what had happened. He earned the nickname "Old Hickory" from his days as a general fighting the British in the war of 1812. His troops revered him, and they often claimed he was as tough as "old hickory wood" on the battlefield. Jackson was a bold military commander who was unafraid to take risks. And in the instant that Lawrence pointed his pistol and pulled the trigger, Jackson was not afraid to leap into action. While Lawrence shouted and ranted in a rage, Jackson threw himself at the man and commenced beating him with his cane.

While Jackson wrestled with his attacker, several congressmen and congressional aides attempted to intervene. One of

THE CORRUPT BARGAIN

Andrew Jackson was no stranger to controversy. In 1824, Jackson lost the presidential election to John Quincy Adams. It was a closely contested election. While Jackson won the popular vote, neither he, Adams, nor Senator Henry Clay won enough electoral votes to claim victory. Under the still-untested Constitution, it was up to the House of Representatives to decide the next president.

While the House debated the candidates' political future, the three each worked their connections in an attempt to sway votes. Eventually Henry Clay decided to throw his support behind John Quincy Adams. With that move, Adams secured enough electoral votes to be elected president. Clay became secretary of state in Adams's cabinet. Jackson was outraged at the outcome of this arrangement. He flew into a rage and accused Adams and Clay of making a "Corrupt Bargain." Jackson threatened to stage a military coup and to create a government in exile in Nashville. There was civil unrest as people rioted over the results of the election.

Eventually Jackson's protests quieted down. John Quincy Adams served one term as president and was defeated by Jackson in the 1828 presidential election. Jackson successfully rebelled against the eastern political dynasties that had controlled American politics since the country's founding. Jackson's rise to power created a new political dynasty as his followers and supporters became known as Jacksonians.

them was the famed frontiersman Davy Crockett, who was serving a term in Congress at the time. He managed to pull Jackson away from Lawrence and hustle the president into a carriage, which drove him to safety.

★ ★ ★

Richard Lawrence, who painted houses for a living, had engaged in odd behavior for many years. He said outsiders were interfering in his life. He told family and relatives that everyone from strangers to the government was preventing him from traveling and earning money rightfully his. He also believed he was Richard III, an English king from the fifteenth century. At other times he suffered from the delusion that he was a wealthy British nobleman who was owed money by the United States.

In time he came to believe President Jackson and his policies regarding national banks were responsible for his problems. At some point he concluded that Jackson needed to die. Then Vice President Martin Van Buren could become president and release the funds Lawrence believed he was owed.

One of the complaints about Jackson from his rivals was his "common man" approach to the presidency. Jackson truly believed the White House was the "People's House," and he allowed ordinary citizens to come and go pretty much as they wished. In the Jackson White House, there were often parties attended by revelers during all hours of the day. Security as we know it today was virtually nonexistent then. This worked to Lawrence's advantage, and he began following Jackson to learn the president's patterns and schedule. He stalked the capital and observed the activity at the White House, watching Jackson's movements at all times

At his trial, Lawrence acted and spoke as if he were a king. He repeatedly told the jurors that he was above them. They could not pass judgment on him. Only he had the authority to pass judgment. His testimony was marked with numerous rants and speeches that demonstrated his flawed mental state. It took the jury only a few minutes of deliberations to find him not guilty by reason of insanity. Lawrence spent the rest of his life in a mental institution.

Jackson's luck in surviving the attempt on his life was truly remarkable. The weather (it was a damp, humid day) may have contributed to his luck. The pistols chosen by Lawrence were notorious for problems with moisture. Still, it was later determined that the odds of both pistols misfiring were 125,000 to 1.

Andrew Jackson survived the battlefield, took a bullet in a duel, and once knocked out a drunk with a bucket. It's only logical he would be shot at, at point-blank range, twice, and survive. He was Old Hickory, after all.

3

THE BALTIMORE PLOT

TODAY HE IS REVERED.

Most historians view him as our greatest president. He is given credit for shepherding the nation through its worst period, the American Civil War.

Yet when he was elected, he was *despised* by fully 50 percent of the population. States voted to secede from the Union rather than remain with him as president. And on his way to Washington, DC, for his inauguration, the sixteenth president's closest advisors learned of a plot to assassinate him.

The Southern response to Abraham Lincoln's November 1860 election was swift and immediate. South Carolina became the first state to attempt to secede from the Union. The other Southern states soon followed suit. The Confederate States of America was born. Through it all Lincoln tried to be reasonable, but he warned the Southern states that secession was not allowed under the Constitution and he would "spare no measure" to preserve the Union.

As March 1861 and Lincoln's inauguration day approached, the country was ready to explode. Even in the North, among Lincoln's supporters, there was disagreement over what should be done about the Southern states. Some said let them go. If they no longer wanted to be part of the United States, they were more than welcome to strike out on their own. Others agreed with Lincoln and believed strongly that the Union must be preserved. Even if it required the use of military force. At a speech in Trenton to the New Jersey General Assembly, Lincoln said, "I shall do all that may be in my power to promote a peaceful settlement of all our difficulties. The man does not live who is more devoted to peace than I am. None who would do more to preserve it. But it may be necessary to put the foot down firmly. And if I do my duty, and do right, you will sustain me, will you not?"

As Lincoln prepared to leave Springfield, Illinois, for Washington, DC, he made plans to stop at more than seventy cities along the way to give speeches and to thank his supporters. His planned stops and schedule of appearances were made public and published in several newspapers. It was this shared information that gave those who would oppose Lincoln the beginnings of their assassination plan. In fact, the information put out to the public was so detailed that it revealed Lincoln's schedule by the minute in some cases.

Lincoln's route would take him by train through Baltimore, Maryland. This was the only way to reach the capital by rail. The problem was that Maryland was a hotbed of Southern sympathizers. It was one of the "border states" that straddled the North and the South, and the citizens of Maryland were sharply divided on the question of slavery. For the time being, they remained in the Union. But the threat that Maryland might secede was never far away.

Baltimore was a choke point in Lincoln's trip to Washington. He would have to disembark at one station and then take a carriage or ride in a rail car pulled by horses to another rail station across town for his DC departure. Either way, the mile-long trip through Baltimore would leave him open and exposed to anyone who might consider doing the president-elect harm.

Lincoln's closest advisors used spies and undercover operatives to unmask the plot circulating among the Southern-sympathizing firebrands of Baltimore. The radical Southern backers were more than capable of carrying out an attack. These were some of the most ardent supporters of slavery, and they were consumed by their hatred for Lincoln.

The task for gathering intelligence on the plot fell to Allan Pinkerton of the Pinkerton National Detective Agency. Pinkerton was already becoming famous for his exploits as a detective. He built his business working mostly in security for the railroads. And it was a perceived threat to the railroad that brought him into protecting Lincoln from the Baltimore plot against the future president's life.

Having learned of the existence of several anti-Union elements in the city, Pinkerton set to work uncovering the details of the plot. He sent detectives in disguise to meet with suspects and went undercover himself, making contact with elements of the conspiracy. Pinkerton found his way into the inner circle of a group of Southern sympathizers by passing himself off as a Southern patriot, determined that Lincoln would not sit in the Oval Office. One of Pinkerton's operatives, Henry Davies, infiltrated another group, even going so far as to take part in a secret initiation. After several weeks of covert work, Pinkerton was convinced the conspirators believed in their cause. Furthermore, he concluded that they were more than capable of carrying out the threat and that steps must be taken to safeguard the president-elect.

As Lincoln traveled through the Northern states and cities, his advisors continued gathering evidence that a plot to assassinate him was in the planning stages. Pinkerton pleaded with Lincoln to change his schedule and—especially in Baltimore—travel mostly at night. At first, Lincoln steadfastly refused to alter his travel plans. Pinkerton instructed his detectives to continue to gather information on any suspected plots. All the while, as the train moved through the cities and countryside of the North, Lincoln continued getting death threats. Some said they would poison, stab, or shoot him; one person promised a venomous spider–filled dumpling.

The word on Lincoln's potential fate was circulating farther and farther. Back in Washington, Senator William Seward, whom Lincoln would name his secretary of state, received information from his son, Frederick, about a plot against Lincoln. Seward ordered Frederick to depart Washington immediately and find Lincoln wherever he was. It would fall on the young Seward to help convince Lincoln to alter his plans.

The challenge would be getting Lincoln to agree.

Young Seward caught up with the Lincoln entourage in

DETECTIVE ALLAN PINKERTON

By the spring of 1861, Allan Pinkerton had become the greatest detective in America. His Pinkerton National Detective Agency was well known for protecting railroads and its hard line during strikes and labor disputes. Pinkerton was born in Scotland, and ironically had to flee the country when his involvement in local political protests led to a price being put on his head. When Pinkerton settled outside Chicago, he began work as a cooper. Pinkerton was an ardent abolitionist, and his barrel-making shop became a stop on the Underground Railroad, helping escaped slaves make their way to freedom in the North.

Pinkerton became a detective for the Chicago City Police force. When the Civil War started, Pinkerton took charge of the Union Army's intelligence service. He used a network of undercover operatives throughout the South to gather information on Confederate troop movements and military installations. Pinkerton even assumed an undercover alias as a Union officer. He was once nearly captured in Memphis and barely escaped with his life.

When President Lincoln took office, he asked Pinkerton to form a secret service, which became tasked with stopping currency counterfeiters and eventually took responsibility

for the safety of the president and first family and other government officials. Pinkerton died in Chicago on July 1, 1884.

Philadelphia. Along with Kate Warne, Allan Pinkerton, and Ward Hill Lamon—Lincoln's former law partner, who had become the president-elect's de facto bodyguard—the group sat Lincoln down for a tense and sometimes confrontational discussion. All of them wanted Lincoln to take precautions to avoid the potential danger. Lincoln had other ideas. Pinkerton urged Lincoln to leave for Washington immediately to throw off the schedule. Lincoln refused, saying, "I cannot go tonight. I have promised to raise the flag over Independence Hall tomorrow morning, and to visit the legislature at Harrisburg in the afternoon—beyond that I have no engagements. Any plan that may be adopted that will enable me to fulfill these promises I will accede to, and you can inform me what is concluded upon tomorrow."

The president-elect found the idea of deception and trickery to be distasteful. He felt that sneaking into Washington, DC, "like a thief in the night" would make him appear weak. It would give ammunition to his opponents, who thought his presidency was already illegitimate. Pinkerton, Seward, and the rest, along with his wife, Mary Todd Lincoln, grew more forceful in their

KATE WARNE—AMERICA'S FIRST WOMAN DETECTIVE

Kate Warne surprised Allan Pinkerton when she answered an ad he'd placed in a Chicago newspaper, looking for detectives. He thought she came to his office to interview for clerical work.

The idea of hiring a woman as a detective was without precedent. But in a preview of how she would approach the job, Kate Warne convinced Pinkerton that she was a perfect choice to be a detective. Women can go places men cannot, she argued. They can win the favor of men and the trust of the wives and girlfriends of criminals. Women are astute observers of human nature and behavior, all qualities a detective needs. Her well-reasoned arguments swayed Pinkerton, and he hired her as the first woman detective in American history.

Kate Warne became one of Pinkerton's best operatives. True to her word, she was able to infiltrate criminal gangs and win the trust of thieves and killers. She was adept at disguises and would even on occasion disguise herself as a young Union soldier. During that period, only men served in the military. Pinkerton and Warne would often travel together, pretending to be husband and wife. And she was an essential operative in foiling the Baltimore plot to assassinate Lincoln.

Before president-elect Lincoln traveled through Baltimore, Warne spent weeks undercover in the city, seeking out secessionist sympathizers and gathering intelligence. Her efforts were instrumental in getting Lincoln safely through to Washington.

After the Civil War, Warne continued working for Pinkerton as his Superintendent of Female Detectives. She continued to work in several high-profile cases and helped Pinkerton grow the Pinkerton National Detective Agency to the foremost detective agency in the world. She died on January 28, 1868, from complications due to pneumonia.

arguments. Lincoln would not be able to fulfill his promise to preserve the Union if he were not alive. They urged Lincoln to travel through Baltimore overnight and depart for Washington without delay.

Lincoln finally agreed to enter the city and make the train transfer at night. After his meeting with Seward, Pinkerton, and the others, Lincoln went on to his scheduled activities in Philadelphia before heading off to meet the Pennsylvania State Legislature at the state capitol in Harrisburg. Pinkerton and the others jumped into action. They had to find a way to get Lincoln safely to and through Baltimore.

Kate Warne took the lead.

Taking responsibility for the Philadelphia-to-Baltimore portion of the trip, she booked passage on the Baltimore train. Warne reserved several sleeping compartments at the rear of the train, concocting a story that she was traveling with her invalid brother who was suffering from an illness. Her brother would stay confined to his berths, and she asked that he not be disturbed since he required quiet and privacy. She may have bribed a conductor on the train to steer other passengers away from the rear sleeping berths.

In Harrisburg, for his trip to the train station, Lincoln departed the hotel dressed in a cloak and a funky-looking wool hat to hide his features. Pinkerton and Lamon also instructed him to walk with a stooped gait, to disguise his height. Pinkerton took the precaution of having the telegraph lines out of Harrisburg cut. This would prevent any conspirators from passing information back and forth. After a carriage ride to the train station, Lincoln boarded unchallenged. Pinkerton spent the trip alternating between Lincoln's side and riding on the rear platform keeping an eye on the tracks behind them. All through the night, either Pinkerton or Lamon remained at the president-elect's side.

Pinkerton had the railroad use just two cars on the train, which was unusual and could attract attention. Each time the train stopped for water, they waited in silence, hoping Lincoln would not be discovered. In fact, soon the engineers discovered that the "rail splitter" was on the train. They were warned to keep quiet and did so. In the rear compartment, no lanterns were lit, on the off chance someone might spot the president-elect. The train made the passage from Harrisburg to Philadelphia without incident.

Both Pinkerton and Warne remarked later that Lincoln remained unusually calm during the trip. He made jokes and tried to sleep, but he was too tall and could not fit comfortably in the bed of his sleeping berth. When the train arrived in Philadelphia, it was early. This also created problems for Pinkerton. He didn't want Lincoln waiting idly at either train station, where he could easily be recognized. Pinkerton decided that the safest approach was to keep the president-elect in a constantly moving carriage. The driver was given vague instructions to drive "northward" until the extra time had passed, then depart for the Pennsylvania, Wilmington & Baltimore Railroad depot. Upon arriving at the platform, Lincoln boarded, and the train departed two minutes later for the four-and-a-half-hour trip to Baltimore.

If Pinkerton was tense on the way to Philadelphia, the trip to Baltimore had him ready to shoot someone. He and Ward Lamon were armed, and Pinkerton made certain his pistol was at the ready. There was nothing to do now but carry on. The motto of the Pinkerton Detective Agency is "We Never Sleep," and it may very well have been invented on that lonely trip to Baltimore. There would be no sleep for Pinkerton and the others on this night.

Finally, the train arrived. Pinkerton waited anxiously while Lincoln's car was uncoupled and hitched to a team of horses that would pull it to the station across the city. At that time of night,

Baltimore was quiet. Pinkerton kept watch and strained to hear for the approach of any group or individuals who might be a threat. The quiet was unnerving, and the minutes ticked slowly past.

Halfway through the trip, the voices of drunken revelers singing "Dixie" could be heard in the distance. The sound made Pinkerton tense with worry.

Then the plan nearly fell apart.

The southbound train that was to carry Lincoln to Washington was late. As the night passed and the threat of a sunrise approached, Pinkerton grew anxious at the delay. From a tactical standpoint they were in a pickle. The closer to dawn, the more people would arrive at the station, ready to begin the day. If Lincoln was recognized and a mob formed, Pinkerton and Ward Lamon were all that stood between the president-elect and his potential murderers. They were isolated, with no way to call for reinforcements or help of any kind. Every plan they considered, from taking a carriage to making the rest of the way on horseback, was deemed too risky.

In the end there was nothing to do but wait.

The minutes ticked by.

People straggled into the station.

Lincoln remained hidden in the rear of the train.

Pinkerton passed the time in near agony.

The sky grew lighter.

More passengers filed into the station, intent on catching early-morning trains.

A train whistle sounded. It was the southbound train. Pinkerton was relieved, but he knew the president-elect and his entourage were not safe yet. They kept the car dark and the curtains drawn, carefully avoiding other passengers.

The president-elect's protectors were on high alert as the car containing Lincoln was coupled to the southbound train and then departed in the predawn hours.

Finally, at six a.m., the train pulled into Washington, DC. Lincoln had arrived safely. Unfortunately, when news of his method of travel leaked out, the response unfolded just as Lincoln feared. Anti-Republican newspapers and especially newspapers in the South made ruthless fun of the new president. Cartoons and illustrations depicted Lincoln as a coward, hiding out in barns and freight cars as he made his way into the capital.

Even members of his own party were embarrassed at the thought of how Lincoln reached Washington. Prominent Republican lawyer and diarist George Templeton Strong wrote, "It's to be hoped that the conspiracy can be proved beyond cavil. If it cannot be made manifest and indisputable, this surreptitious nocturnal dodging or sneaking of the president-elect into his capital city, under cloud of night, will be used to damage his moral position and throw ridicule on his Administration." Critics assailed Lincoln, claiming he had snuck into town disguised in a kilt and other outrageous outfits. Others ridiculed Lincoln for making the trip and leaving his family to travel the more dangerous route alone.

Still, Pinkerton had no regrets. He and his detectives had saved the president-elect. The how of it mattered not to him. Years later he wrote: "I had informed Mr. Lincoln in Philadelphia that I would answer with my life for his safe arrival in Washington, and I had redeemed my pledge."

4

FIRST YOU GET SHOT, THEN YOU GIVE A SPEECH

"I DON'T KNOW WHETHER you fully understand that I have just been shot. But it takes more than that to kill a Bull Moose."

He had a reputation for being a tough guy.

He loved wrestling, boxing, riding horses, and going hunting.

But on October 14, 1912, he might have shown a will few men could match. About to give a speech, Teddy Roosevelt asked the audience for quiet. Slowly he unbuttoned his vest. Beneath it lay a bloodstained shirt. Reaching into his suit coat pocket, he removed a fifty-page document—a copy of his speech for the evening. It was torn and rent by bullets. Roosevelt spoke to the assembled crowd. "Fortunately, I had my manuscript, so you see I was going to make a long speech, and there is a bullet—there is where the bullet went through—and it probably saved me from it going into my heart. The bullet is in me now, so that I cannot make a very long speech, but I will try my best."

The bullet was in him.

He went on to speak for nearly ninety minutes, refusing several times to be taken to the hospital until he was finished.

Minutes before, Roosevelt had been traveling to the auditorium in an open-air automobile. As he left his hotel and stepped into the car that evening, a would-be assassin rushed forward. He fired a single shot, striking Roosevelt in the chest. The gunman was wrestled to the ground before he could shoot again.

★ ★ ★

From the time he was a small child, Roosevelt had challenged himself to excel, both physically and mentally. He suffered from asthma and was extremely nearsighted. He also had a father who wanted a "rugged son" and was disappointed in young Teddy's frailty. As a result, Teddy spent his life doing a lot of dangerous things trying to prove how tough he was.

Roosevelt called it living a "strenuous life." With his father's help he built a gym in his home and began lifting weights and taking boxing lessons. He worked out daily, willing his sickly body to improve.

Roosevelt was a president unlike most others. He was incredibly popular. Throughout American history presidents have been both loved and loathed. At any given time, fully half of the country has a negative opinion of the current president. But Roosevelt transcended this. He traveled extensively during political campaigns and thousands of people of all political stripes turned out to see him.

Before he entered politics, Roosevelt went about living a

"strenuous life." When he enrolled at Harvard, he took up competitive rowing and running. After dropping out of law school, Roosevelt went to South Dakota and lived the life of a rancher. He bought a large cattle ranch and spent two years as a cowboy until he finally returned to the East Coast. Teddy served in the New York State legislature and held a variety of other political offices before he was chosen to serve as the vice presidential candidate to William McKinley.

Everything Roosevelt did, he did with energy and passion. When it came to campaigning, he simply outworked everyone. In the 1912 presidential election campaign he visited thirty-eight states (remember this is an age before commercial airlines). His speeches were always well attended, with hundreds and thousands of people turning out to see him.

With William Howard Taft running as a Republican and Woodrow Wilson running as a Democrat, Roosevelt decided to run as a third-party candidate when he grew disillusioned with Taft. Taft had served as Roosevelt's vice president. But Roosevelt was frustrated with Taft's administration.

There was a tradition that presidents would only serve two terms. But Roosevelt decided to seek the Republican nomination. When his attempt failed, and the Republican Party denied him the nomination, he formed the National Progressive Party—which became known as the Bull Moose Party.

Now a constitutional amendment prevents presidents from serving more than two terms. But in 1912, Teddy Roosevelt threw himself into the campaign to serve a third time.

★ ★ ★

Roosevelt had already given several speeches on the same day as the assassination attempt. Milwaukee was the third city he'd visited in the previous twelve hours. He was tired and losing his voice. The would-be assassin, John Flammang Schrank, had been following Roosevelt across the country, waiting for his opportunity to strike as Roosevelt left the hotel. Schrank fired his pistol directly into Roosevelt's chest from a distance of about five feet.

Chaos ensued.

Several of Roosevelt's aides jumped into action. Schrank was quickly subdued and prevented from firing the gun again. When the crowd realized what had happened, they began to shout for Schrank's head. Roosevelt called for order and to have Schrank brought to him. "Don't hurt him. Bring him here. I want to see him." Roosevelt spoke directly to Schrank, "What did you do it for?" Schrank did not answer. "Oh, what's the use? Turn him over to the police," Roosevelt said. Schrank was hauled away, with the crowd demanding he be hanged on the spot.

An experienced big-game hunter, Roosevelt took this opportunity to spit into his hand. There was no blood in his spittle. From this, he realized the bullet had not pierced a lung. This was good news, as it meant it was likely not a life-threatening bullet wound. Just a scratch. In fact, feeling around his shirt, probing the wound, Roosevelt said, "He pinked me."

Roosevelt insisted that he be taken to the auditorium to give his speech rather than to the hospital for treatment. Ironically, Roosevelt had assumed the presidency when an assassin shot President William McKinley. Now his aides and assistants tried to overrule him, insisting he go to the hospital straightaway. Roosevelt probably stared them down and reminded them that he was the boss. He was going to give his speech. No one, not even an assassin, was going to stop him.

In fact, after Roosevelt told the crowd he had been shot and it would take more than a single bullet to topple a Bull Moose, he reminded them, "Now, friends, I am not speaking for myself at all, I give you my word, I do not care a rap about being shot; not a rap."

Roosevelt attacked the speech as if he were leading another charge up San Juan Hill. His aides and bodyguards nervously hovered near him on the podium in case he faltered. But he did not. The crowd was spellbound. At the conclusion of his address, he received a rousing ovation.

After the speech was finished, Roosevelt was hustled to a nearby hospital. X-rays showed that the bullet had lodged in his chest beneath a broken rib and stopped about one inch from his lung. Lucky for him that he carried his glasses case and his folded speech in his suit pocket. And that his aides had wrestled the gun away from the assassin Schrank before he could fire another shot.

After examining Roosevelt, doctors determined it was safer to leave the bullet where it was. There would be no surgery to remove it. It remained in his chest for the rest of his life. Roosevelt fully recovered from the wound but needed to suspend his campaign while he healed. He lost the election but gained a hunk of lead as a souvenir. Roosevelt never ran for office again. He went on to become an author, explorer, and hunter, always challenging himself to live a strenuous life. He survived war, adventure, and an assassin's bullet.

It takes more than that to kill a Bull Moose.

JOHN FLAMMANG SCHRANK—
THE GHOST TOLD ME TO DO IT

A Bavarian immigrant, John Flammang Schrank suffered several traumas at an early age. Shortly after arriving in the United States at the age of nine, his parents passed away. He went to work for his aunt and uncle who owned a tavern. When they died, they left their properties to Schrank. Tragedy continued to visit him when his girlfriend was killed in a steamboat accident on the East River in New York. When she passed, Schrank sold his properties and became a drifter, moving from town to town along the East Coast.

There is little known about Schrank's activities from the time he sold his properties until his assassination attempt on Theodore Roosevelt. He became known for engaging in debates on biblical topics. He was often seen wandering around city streets at all hours of the night. But there is no documentation of him being in any trouble before trying to kill Roosevelt.

At his trial, Schrank claimed the ghost of President William McKinley spoke to him and told him to kill Roosevelt. Apparently, McKinley's ghost was upset with his former vice president for attempting to win a third term. So he visited Schrank in a dream and instructed him to take out Roosevelt. Happens all the time. At his trial, Schrank was found not guilty by reason of insanity. He was confined to a mental institution, where he died in 1943.

5

A SHOOTOUT WITH THE CAPITOL POLICE

THERE HAVE BEEN MANY attempted assassinations of US presidents. Assassins' bullets have felled four presidents, and several others have narrowly escaped. One of those was President Harry S. Truman, who watched a gunfight unfold in the street below him.

In truth, Truman survived two attempted assassinations. The first was a letter bomb directed at him, but it was intercepted in the White House mail room. Truman was nowhere close by. But the next time, he watched from the second floor of Blair House, where he stayed while the White House was renovated.

★ ★ ★

Harry Truman was a blunt, plainspoken midwesterner. His presidency followed Franklin Delano Roosevelt's twelve years in the

White House. FDR had been elected to an unprecedented fourth term in 1944; no other president had served more than two. With the Great Depression and World War II happening during his presidency, Roosevelt thought he should stay in office to see them through. Shortly after the inauguration for his fourth term, Roosevelt passed away. Truman, FDR's vice president, took office. Truman was in many ways the polar opposite of the East Coast elegant and cerebral Roosevelt. He was temperamental and didn't shy away from a fight.

TRUMAN AND THE BUCK STOPS HERE

President Truman has a historical reputation as a man of great integrity. He became president when Franklin Delano Roosevelt died in office in April 1945, while World War II was still raging. President Truman had to continue Roosevelt's work to ensure an Allied victory. He became notorious for his decision to drop atomic bombs on Hiroshima and Nagasaki in Japan.

These were not decisions Truman took lightly. Many believed that Japan would never surrender. To invade Japan would cost tens of thousands of American lives. Only a massive display of force would bring Japan to heel.

Indeed, after the second bomb dropped on Nagasaki the Japanese surrendered.

Truman took responsibility for his decisions. One of his most famous sayings was "the buck stops here." On his desk in the Oval Office he kept a small wooden sign with the phrase printed on it. It meant that he would not allow himself or his aides to blame others for their decisions.

The phrase "passing the buck" originated from a card game where a marker or "buck" is placed in front of a player to signify that they are the dealer for that hand. After the hand concludes, the "buck is passed" to the next player. It eventually came to mean that someone would try to pass on the responsibility for something they did to someone else. Truman would not allow it.

President Truman was not afraid to fight with either the press or his political rivals. Many believed he would never match Roosevelt against leaders like Winston Churchill of the United Kingdom or Joseph Stalin of the Soviet Union on the world stage. But Truman proved to be more than adequate to the task.

The buck stopped with him.

Truman's would-be killers were motivated by politics to take extreme measures. They were Puerto Rican citizens who wanted independence for their country. They belonged to the Puerto Rican Nationalist Party (PRNP).

The two men were named Oscar Collazo and Griselo Torresola. On October 31, 1950, they traveled by train from New York City to Washington, DC. Their goal was to assassinate the president and bring attention to the cause of Puerto Rican independence. On October 30, the PRNP leader had launched several attacks against US military personnel on the island of Puerto Rico. The next stage of their plan was to kill the president, which would gain worldwide headlines for the PRNP.

The US military made a swift and ferocious response to the PRNP attacks in Puerto Rico. Collazo and Torresola knew that they were undertaking a suicide mission. The Secret Service protecting Truman would be on high alert. They pledged to each other that they would go down fighting.

Collazo later said he was not familiar with guns, nor was he a very good shot. Torresola had purchased a P38 and a German Luger to use in their attack. He had to give Collazo a quick lesson in how to operate the guns.

According to Secret Service reports, the two men awoke early and dressed in newly purchased suits. They went sightseeing that morning and discovered that President Truman was not living in the White House. While it was undergoing renovations, he occupied Blair House. A five-minute walk from the White House, Blair House serves as the president's guest house. The fact that Truman was staying there may have played a role in his survival of the attack unharmed.

Almost every day, Truman would leave the Oval Office and return to Blair House to have lunch with his wife, Bess. After lunch he would take a short nap. Truman was a believer in the power of naps. It was part of his midwestern charm.

While Truman had fallen asleep upstairs, Collazo and Torresola departed their cab and walked up and down the street several times, studying Blair House. They took notice of the doors and windows and observed four men standing at the house front. The four were divided between two small guard booths.

Collazo proved his incompetence in handling firearms. He sneaked up behind White House police officer Donald Birdzell, pointed the gun at his head, and pulled the trigger. Just as with Andrew Jackson's assassin, the gun did not fire. But it made a loud noise, alerting Birdzell to his attacker's presence. Unlike with Jackson, this was a modern revolver, not a gunpowder-fired, single-shot pistol. There was a second bullet waiting. Collazo pulled the trigger. The bullet struck Birdzell in his knee, and he went down.

The gunfire set the Secret Service and the White House police into action. Several agents poured out of Blair House, firing at Collazo and knocking him down. He was out of the gunfight, but his wounds would not kill him.

At the eastern end of the property, Torresola sprayed the building with bullets. Leslie Coffelt was another White House policeman on duty at Blair House. Torresola ambushed the officer. With the German Luger, Torresola, who was a much better shot than Collazo, shot Coffelt in the chest three times. Coffelt would succumb to his wounds, making him the first and only member of a presidential protective detail (including the Secret Service) to be killed in the line of duty.

47

After the fight started, the president himself peered out the window to see what all the commotion was about. The guards yelled at him to get down, and he ducked back inside Blair House. At the exact moment Harry Truman decided it would be a good idea to stick his head out the window, Torresola was reloading and was preoccupied. If not for that, given Torresola's skill with firearms, the president could have been killed or wounded. Instead, Officer Coffelt was not quite done yet. Somehow, he found the strength and shot Torresola, killing him before succumbing to his own wounds. The president was saved. It was the longest gun battle in White House police history. The entire incident took less than a minute.

The next year Congress passed legislation increasing the Secret Service's protection duties. It was this assassination attempt that created today's modern Secret Service. Collazo was sentenced to death, but Truman commuted his sentence to life in prison. Collazo was released in 1994 when President Carter commuted his sentence. He returned to Puerto Rico and died there that year.

President Truman went on to finish out his term as president. Luckily the buck didn't stop there.

I DON'T LIKE IKE

DURING WORLD WAR II there was a popular saying—"loose lips sink ships."

It was part of a wartime informational campaign to remind the public that enemy spies could be anywhere. With so many people mobilized and working in the defense industry, information in the wrong hands could be a real danger. These campaigns were called propaganda, and they were a way for governments to influence the public to support the war effort. They were used for everything from encouraging citizens to buy war bonds to warning about spies and conspiracies.

Before he was the thirty-fourth president of the United States, General Dwight David Eisenhower served in World War II as the Supreme Commander of the Allied troops in Europe. Under his leadership, the American, British, Canadian, and other forces defeated the Axis Powers in Europe, composed primarily of Nazi Germany and Italy. While in the United States Army, Eisenhower approved plans to allow African American servicemen to integrate in the armed forces. Later, as president, one of the most noted accomplishments of his presidency was to send the US Army into Little Rock, Arkansas, to make sure their schools followed the law and allowed African American students to attend them.

But before Eisenhower was president, it was a group of black Americans on guard duty who helped thwart a Nazi plan to assassinate him. It was a daring gamble by the Nazi command. During the Battle of the Bulge in Belgium, they intended to send English-speaking German soldiers dressed as American GIs behind the US lines to destroy bridges, spring ambushes, and try to assassinate the High Command of the Allied army, including General Eisenhower.

★ ★ ★

The Battle of the Bulge was a back-and-forth affair. The front lines became a confusing muddle of two giant armies hammering each other. Often, neither the Allied nor the German forces had any idea where the front was, and in the confusion of war, they could easily find themselves behind each other's lines. The battle was also fought in the middle of a brutally cold winter, which made it even harder to keep track of enemy positions.

As often happens with front-line forces, rumors of German activities and troop movements burned through the corps, but actual intelligence was hard to come by. American soldiers heard everything from German commandos dropping paratroopers into England to free prisoners of war to spies behind enemy lines cutting telephone wires and blowing up bridges. None of it was true. What was true is that Adolf Hitler had launched a desperate plan, using his best special forces soldier, to strike at the American and British High Command. That soldier's name was Otto Skorzeny.

Skorzeny was a Nazi officer who developed the German army's techniques for operating among the enemy and other covert activities. He participated in a mission to free the Italian dictator Benito Mussolini from captivity by flying gliders high into the Italian mountains. Mussolini had been arrested by the Italian government and had his power taken away. Hitler sent his crack troops, including Skorzeny, to rescue him.

Most everyone in the German High Command knew that Germany was likely to lose the war. The Battle of the Bulge would be their last serious attempt to smash the Allied army. Skorzeny came up with the idea of sending English-speaking German soldiers behind enemy lines. They would be dressed in American uniforms, carry counterfeit US money, and do whatever they could to disrupt the American and British advance. And there are some sources, including Skorzeny himself, that claim their mission was to try to reach the Allied headquarters in France and kidnap or kill General Eisenhower and other top leaders.

German soldiers who could speak English were selected and trained for the mission. They were all volunteers. That was because if they were caught, they would be executed. Armies tend to take a dim view of spies. Especially spies who dress to look like their adversaries, which makes it hard to know whom to shoot.

The sinister plan was code named Operation Greif—Operation Grip. Those soldiers selected for the mission practiced their English. They even went into American POW camps to learn current slang. American uniforms, weapons, and captured vehicles were gathered up and restored for use. To further their efforts, the Nazi government also printed counterfeit US currency. They hoped using the fake bills would create confusion and suspicion among American soldiers.

With everything in place and the Battle of the Bulge fully under way, it was time for Operation Greif to commence. It is not known exactly how many German agents were involved—numbers from different sources vary, but there were several teams. And in December 1945 they made their way toward the American lines.

★   ★   ★

On the morning of December 18, 1945, a jeep approached a checkpoint at a small bridge in the village of Aywaille, deep in the Ardennes forest of Belgium. The bridge was guarded by a unit of American Military Police and a group of African American soldiers. The Germans had already made a crucial mistake. One thing the Germans didn't understand about the American military was the huge quantity of equipment America used in the war effort. Jeeps were so plentiful it was unusual to see one carrying more than two passengers. This jeep had three men in it. The MPs ordered it to stop.

The American soldiers were on edge. They had heard rumors about German commandos penetrating Allied lines. Stories about communication lines being cut, bridges being blown up, and dozens of other rumors were rampant.

When the jeep rolled to a stop at the bridge, a military policeman demanded to know that day's password. According to witnesses of the event, the driver muttered something unintelligible. The MP insisted they provide the password. It was standard protocol. Each morning before departing their units, soldiers were given the day's password. When the spy soldiers were unable to comply, the MPs ordered them out of the jeep.

This was part of the brilliance of Skorzeny's plan. Giving the enemy false or misleading information is a common and effective tactic in warfare. It has been used by armies for centuries. All over the front lines, legitimate American soldiers were being detained and questioned, simply because someone on guard duty was nervous and suspicious. Rank didn't matter either. General Bruce Clarke was arrested and detained because a guard told him that he had heard the Germans were sending an imposter one-star general into the American lines. To the guard, Clarke "didn't look right." Even Field Marshal Bernard Montgomery, the commander of all British forces, was grilled relentlessly when he passed through checkpoints.

The men were searched. The three men gave their names as Private First-Class Charles W. Lawrence, Private First-Class George Sensenbach, and Private First-Class Clarence van der Werth. They all seemed like "regular Joes." The African American soldiers inspected the jeep and discovered the deception. Among the equipment in the jeep were rolls of one-hundred-dollar bills. It was part of the massive amount of counterfeit currency the Germans had printed.

The African American soldiers fell upon the jeep. Inside it they found dozens of British and American weapons and machine pistols, even American grenades. They even had cigarette lighters containing poison. The three men were detained, and the MPs placed a call to headquarters. The news sent the Allied commanders into a frenzy. Jeeploads of MPs and counterintelligence officers descended on the bridge. The three men were taken into custody and interrogated.

When questioned, the three men revealed they had penetrated American lines about a week earlier posing as members of the Fifth Armored Division. Their specific mission was to observe the conditions of bridges and report back. The men must have known they would be executed as spies and probably hoped they would be spared if they cooperated. They couldn't talk fast enough.

One of the men revealed he was one of the first to join an organization created by Otto Skorzeny. His training had taken place at the SS camp at Friedenthal. The big shocker came when he revealed that teams of commandos and combat engineers were trying to make their way to Allied headquarters in France, where they would either blow up the building or enter and kill as many of the High Command as possible. The ultimate goal was to kill Eisenhower.

The American counterintelligence operatives were sent into a frenzy. They believed Skorzeny himself was somewhere behind their lines, directing the operation. That he was personally involved in a plot to kill General Eisenhower. All over the American lines, soldiers became convinced that everyone was a German spy. Even General Omar Bradley, second in command to Eisenhower, was not spared. "Three times I was ordered to prove my identity by cautious GIs. The first time by identifying Springfield as the capital of Illinois (my questioner held out for

Chicago); the second time by locating the guard between the center and tackle on a line of scrimmage; the third time by naming the then current spouse of a blonde named Betty Grable. Grable stopped me, but the sentry did not. Pleased at having stumped me, he nevertheless passed me on. A half million GIs played cat and mouse with each other each time they met on the road. Neither rank nor credentials spared the traveler an inquisition at each intersection he passed."

Skorzeny had become the devil, the bogeyman, and a ghost, all wrapped up into one. What the Americans didn't know was that Skorzeny was indeed behind American lines (against Hitler's orders) but had been wounded and returned to Berlin for treatment. Skorzeny turned himself over to the Americans in May 1945, as the war in Europe drew to a close.

If this plan to assassinate Eisenhower was real and had worked, it would have been a great moral and political victory for Germany. It might not have changed the outcome, but it might have prolonged the war. Skorzeny was tried as a war criminal and found not guilty. He was debriefed by US intelligence agencies because of his knowledge about the Soviet Union, and later he went on to become a military advisor for both Egypt and Israel.

Many years later, a writer interviewed Skorzeny in Germany. He was asked if he had really implemented a plan to kill General Eisenhower. His answer was as mysterious as the frenzy he caused behind American lines in 1944. He said, "I shall not answer that directly. But you must believe this, if I had intended to kill Ike, I would have done so."

We will never know. Luckily Eisenhower lived, and Germany was defeated.

7

PT-109

IT WAS A BAD night to be on the water.

The sky was cloudy and moonless. Fog rolled in over the strait. The other PT boats were invisible in the settling gloom. Still, the enemy was out there. Somewhere. They were certain of it. Destroyers. Maybe battleships. All of them bristling with guns and torpedoes.

The small craft bobbed gently on the waves. It was set to silent running, one muffled engine quietly idling in the pitch-black night. The crew was anxious. Every noise, any sound, no matter how muted, could alert the Japanese that swarmed these islands. And if that happened, they would be vastly outnumbered.

In command of PT-109 was Lieutenant (Junior Grade) John F. Kennedy. Like the rest of the crew, he was antsy. He had wanted to serve in combat since the war began. Being in command of a PT boat would not have been his first choice. PT boats did not have a great record in the fight up to that point. The typical Japanese warship had guns and torpedoes with far greater range. PT boats could outrun them, but they needed to get in close to fire their torpedoes, well within range of enemy weapons. Firing the torpedoes in the darkness would also give away their position, making them vulnerable to return fire from enemy ships and aircraft. Sitting on the open water, waiting to engage a bigger, more heavily armed foe, tended to make the captain and crew a little nervous.

They did everything in their power to remain hidden. The slowly idling single engine would leave no wake that could be spotted by on-shore artillery or from the sky above by Japanese planes. The motors were muffled to reduce noise. Somewhere out on the water, two other PT boats waited, but in the darkness, they were no longer visible.

The PTs were cruising the waters near Kolombangara Island in the South Pacific. PT-109 had been assigned to search for Japanese warships that were delivering men and supplies to bases in the area. So far, they had no luck. They had been in these waters for some time. No ships had appeared. It looked as if the Japanese navy had succeeded with their nightly resupply of troops and supplies to the island.

Up ahead, without warning, a dark and shadowy shape appeared, slicing through the gloom. It was a Japanese warship headed right for them. From the forward machine-gun turret came a shout: "Ship at two o'clock!"

There was little time to act.

The crew had less than ten seconds to get the engines to full speed and evade the destroyer. There was no time to load or fire rounds from the .37 mm gun. The destroyer, later determined to be the *Amagiri*, hit PT-109 broadside. It cut the ship in two on a diagonal from amidships to the stern. Fuel exploded. Screams filled the air.

The night erupted in fire and smoke.

And for the first of several times over the next few days, John Fitzgerald Kennedy wondered if this was what it felt like to die.

THE DEVIL BOATS

Patrol torpedo (PT) boats were an attempt by the United States to get more firepower quickly into the fight in the Pacific. They were made of wood and could be built faster, which kept regular shipyards free to build steel ships. They were armed with heavy machine guns and each held three powerful Packard engines. There was only one problem with the PT boats.

The torpedoes.

The torpedoes used in the PT fleet were old (many left over from World War I) and tended to misfire with regularity. On the night PT-109 was sunk, the entire PT squadron fired thirty torpedoes at the enemy and caused no damage. It is not even clear if any of the torpedoes detonated.

Only about one-quarter of PT boats in service were equipped with radar. And their crews were not well trained. PTs were fast and maneuverable but not able to easily take on bigger, more heavily armed warships. They were useful for reconnaissance and search-and-rescue operations. In the Solomon Islands, the Japanese used a fleet of barges to resupply their bases, and the PT boats did have success against them. The crews of the barges referred to the PTs as "the devil boats."

Because of their lack of training and ineffective equipment, the PT squadrons were often referred to as "the Hooligan Navy." At the end of the war, the PT program was discontinued. The boats were dismantled or given away to other countries.

Two members of the crew on PT-109 died instantly in the collision. The rest were tossed around the boat or hurled into the water. Kennedy was thrown about the cockpit. Fire was now the greater danger, and Kennedy ordered everyone to abandon ship. Luckily, the *Amagiri*'s wake dispersed the fuel across the water, and it did not ignite.

As his crew floated in the sea, Kennedy assessed the situation. "Who's aboard?" he shouted. "Who's aboard?"

Slowly, the word came back to him. About half the crew was still on the wrecked ship. Part of the hull of PT-109 was still afloat. With the danger of fire past, Kennedy ordered the remaining crew to climb back onto the floating wreck. It would give them a little temporary shelter. They needed to be cautious. These waters were controlled by the Japanese. If they were spotted, they could be captured or executed.

The area was dotted with dozens of tiny islands, several of which were occupied by enemy troops. All through the night the remaining crew huddled on the broken hull of PT-109. At daybreak, Kennedy spotted an island that might offer shelter and water. They would have to swim for it.

One of his men, Machinist's Mate Patrick "Pop" McMahon, was badly burned in the collision and unable to fend for himself. Kennedy helped McMahon into a life jacket. Then he cut a strap loose and put it in his mouth, towing the injured man with his teeth. The rest of the men clutched a piece of the wreckage and splashed their way toward the island. It was small and flat with a few coconut trees, and it was known as Plum Pudding Island.

It was slow going. Kennedy had been a champion swimmer at Harvard. Even towing McMahon, he still felt he could handle the distance. It took several hours to reach the island, and Kennedy arrived before the rest of his crew. Exhausted, he collapsed on the beach. The injured McMahon helped pull him onto the sand, where he fell asleep.

But Kennedy's swimming was not over for the night. This area of the Solomon Islands was swarming with Japanese. He determined the crew was in danger the longer they remained out in the open. He decided to swim to the open water of Ferguson Passage, where the rest of the PT squadron patrolled. Leaving the crew behind on the island, Kennedy made his way across the reef and into the passage. He spent several hours treading water in the dark, but no PT boats appeared.

Kennedy's bad day grew much worse on his return to the island. He was weak and injured from the collision and exhausted from the swimming he'd already done. The currents in this part of the Solomon Islands are extremely fickle. They swirl and twist, and when the tides change, they can play havoc on a boat or ship, let alone a swimmer. On his way back to Plum Pudding Island the exhausted Kennedy was pulled into the grip of the currents. He was tossed and turned in the water, struggling to stay afloat. The water pulled him into Blackett Strait and then back into Ferguson Passage.

After resting for part of the day at another small island, Kennedy finally made the return swim to Plum Pudding Island. He staggered his way onto the beach and collapsed on the sand. Before falling into an exhausted sleep, he ordered Ensign George Ross to swim back out to Ferguson Passage that evening to keep watch for PT boats.

At this point Kennedy and his men expected to be rescued.

But there was no rescue coming.

Everyone thought they were dead.

When the PT-109 was hit, the crews aboard PT-162 and PT-169 saw the massive explosion. Both crews assumed there were no survivors. It was impossible to believe anyone had endured such a fiery crash. Both PTs fired torpedoes at the

Amagiri but missed. The two PTs returned to their base at Rendova and reported the collision.

The men of PT-109 missed their own funerals. At headquarters, memorial services were held for the crew. There were even condolence letters written to a few of the men's families. Meanwhile, the boat's crew sat huddled on their small island, hiding from the Japanese, not realizing there was no one looking for them.

★   ★   ★

Plum Pudding Island was barely one hundred yards in diameter. The supply of coconuts was dwindling; fresh water was becoming critical. The men weren't going to last long on this small hunk of rock. Kennedy decided they would swim to another island that would take them closer to Ferguson Passage.

Back in the water they went. Kennedy towed McMahon again. The rest of the crew splashed through the water with the plank from the wreckage. It had been four days with no fresh water and little food. The new island was larger and about three miles away. When they finally reached the shoreline, they found plentiful coconut trees, which gave them some food and coconut milk to drink.

Kennedy could relax a little. His men were safe and had food. But his injured crewmen were getting worse. They needed medical attention. And the threat of discovery by the Japanese was still there. He needed to find a way to rescue his men.

Considering their options, Kennedy and Ross decided to swim to another island where they thought they might locate friendly natives. They might be able to find a boat or supplies that would help the crew. They set off for the island.

The island was called Nauru. When Kennedy and Ross arrived there, their luck changed entirely. They found a Japanese barge that had gone aground just offshore. Two native men were nearby, but when they spotted the American officers, they took off in a canoe. Exploring the island, Kennedy and Ross found a small shelter in the trees that contained a keg of water. They also discovered a box that contained Japanese candy and hardtack biscuits. The food was like a small feast for the two men. Exploring the island further, they found a small two-person canoe.

They waited until nightfall to avoid any Japanese patrols. Kennedy left Ross on the island and took the canoe out on the water and returned to the island where the crew waited. The men were overjoyed to see their skipper. Kennedy shared the crackers and water.

The next morning Kennedy wanted to return to Nauru, and he set out in the canoe. But the weather changed, and the sea grew rough. The canoe was tossed about on the water. The waves battered the canoe, and once again, Kennedy feared he might drown in the unforgiving sea. Luckily, from out of nowhere, several natives appeared in a canoe and pulled him from the water.

The natives took him back to Nauru, and Kennedy was reunited with Ross. Kennedy found a coconut shell and carved a message into the surface:

NAURO ISL
COMMANDER . . . NATIVE KNOWS
POS'IT . . . HE CAN PILOT . . . 11 ALIVE
NEED SMALL BOAT . . . KENNEDY

Finishing the message, Kennedy gave the coconut to the natives and said, "Rendova. Rendova." Meaning he wanted them to take the coconut to the US base at Rendova. The men appeared to understand and left by canoe with Kennedy's message.

Kennedy and Ross spent the rest of the day recovering. They were weak and sick from malnutrition and swallowing salt water and exhausted from being tossed about by the surf. That evening they took a two-man canoe the natives had left for them out into the passage.

It was a mistake.

The wind came up. The sea rose. The canoe was soon swamped.

All Kennedy and Ross could do was to hang on for dear life.

★ ★ ★

The tide was going out, and the wind was pushing Kennedy and Ross toward the open sea. They clung desperately to the side of the swamped canoe. The currents took them toward an island, and they could hear the waves crashing into a reef. Without warning a huge wave took hold of Kennedy and ripped him away from the canoe. He was spun through the water and thrown against the ocean floor. When the waves finally pushed him onto the reef, the future president was battered and bruised.

Kennedy staggered toward shore, calling for Ross. At first he feared the worst, but Ross finally answered his skipper's shouts. With both of their feet cut and bleeding from the coral reef, the men gingerly made their way to shore. Reaching the sand, they collapsed into an exhausted sleep.

The next morning, they woke to find four natives standing on the shore. The islanders were friendly. One of them spoke English and said to Kennedy, "I have a letter for you, sir." The correspondence was from Lieutenant Wincote of the New Zealand army. Wincote was a coast watcher. These were soldiers who hid out on the islands, often behind enemy lines. They kept an eye on Japanese troop movements and reported when ships and planes were under way to attack American positions.

In his letter, Wincote asked for Kennedy to accompany the natives to his camp. First, though, the natives took Kennedy and Ross back to their men. They cooked a meal for the hungry crew and helped treat the wounds of the injured. The men felt a tremendous sense of relief. Their ordeal was nearly over.

Kennedy climbed into the canoe. The natives covered him with palm fronds in case a passing Japanese boat or plane should spot them. Kennedy met with Lieutenant Wincote and arranged for another PT boat to pick up his crew. That night the boat arrived. They returned to the island and gathered up the crew and roared off to their base. The men were jubilant.

The news of Kennedy's rescue made headlines back in the United States. But he never truly got over the loss of his two crewmen and spent the rest of his time in the Solomon Islands volunteering for dangerous missions. It was as if he wanted revenge against the enemy that had taken his men.

Kennedy's health continued to deteriorate. He was finally ordered home to take physical therapy at a hospital in Arizona. He was discharged from the navy in 1945.

★ ★ ★

The story of PT-109 and Kennedy's heroic actions took on a life of its own. When he ran for president, he told his story to a reporter at the *New Yorker* magazine. That story was reprinted in *Reader's Digest* and reached tens of thousands of readers. A popular song, "PT-109," was written and recorded by singer Jimmy Dean, and a movie, *PT-109*, was released in 1963.

Yet Kennedy had a different take on his experience. The loss of his two crewmen weighed on him for the rest of his life. Like many who survive a horrific combat experience, he did not view himself as especially heroic. Years later he was asked how he felt about becoming a hero in the navy. He replied, "It was involuntary. They sank my boat."

8

THE FALL OF GERALD FORD

SOMETIMES YOU ARE FORCED to save yourself. There isn't anyone around to help. No aide to wrestle an assassin to the ground or squadron mates to pull you out of the sea. Sometimes you have to rely on your own reflexes to not die.

Gerald R. Ford was the thirty-eighth president of the United States. He was the only man to serve as vice president and president without being elected to either office. He had a reputation for being clumsy, often tripping and falling, bumping his head on the doorway of Air Force One and hitting golf balls into crowds. While in office he was made fun of relentlessly by comedians and impressionists for his bumbling demeanor.

True, Ford did fall down a lot. But much of the criticism was unfounded. He was actually an exceptional athlete, playing football at the University of Michigan, as well as an excellent golfer. And he wasn't just a football player at Michigan. He was a star. The University of Michigan had a powerhouse team when Ford attended. He was even named the team's Most Valuable Player. Ford wore the number 48 during his Michigan career, and his jersey was eventually retired by the university.

After his college football career, he was offered contracts to play for the Detroit Lions and the Green Bay Packers as an offensive lineman. Ford declined and instead went to law school. After graduating, he became a practicing attorney in Grand Rapids, Michigan.

But like many men of his generation, the December 7, 1941 attack on Pearl Harbor by Japan interrupted Ford's life trajectory. The future president enlisted in the Navy Reserve. Called to active duty, he was commissioned an ensign and went through training. After several duty stations in the States, Ford requested sea duty. He was assigned to the aircraft carrier USS *Monterey* in the Third Fleet under the command of Admiral William "Bull" Halsey. And it was Halsey's hard-charging style that nearly cost Ford his life in the South Pacific, when Halsey decided to sail the Third Fleet right into the heart of a typhoon.

★ ★ ★

Halsey was forceful and demanding, and he wasn't afraid to mix it up. His motto as a naval commander was "hit first, hit hard, and hit often." Some considered him dangerous and crazy. A man of his times, he was pugnacious, combative, and often used racist words for his Japanese enemy.

When given command of the naval forces in the South Pacific, Halsey took his fleet on a whirlwind of "quick strike" attacks on enemy-held positions. He bombarded several islands, and his fleet was the launch platform for Jimmy Doolittle's famous raid on Tokyo in 1942.

Halsey's aggression fueled the action that nearly ended his career. In December 1944, Halsey's fleet was taking part in maneuvers near the Philippines when a large typhoon began moving into the area. The fleet's ship commanders received conflicting reports about the storm's direction. Halsey decided to keep his ships in place for an extra day. It was a fatal mistake.

CARRIER POWER IN WORLD WAR II

World War II saw many changes in how wars were carried out. Groundbreaking technologies were developed. Especially in the Pacific, with so many islands to fight on, new tactics were required. But there was one innovation that still resonates in the American military today: aircraft carriers.

The airplane was first used widely as a weapon in World War I. After the Great War, the US Navy developed the ability to land and launch a plane from a floating platform. The

USS *Langley* became the navy's first carrier in 1920, after it was converted from a coal-carrying ship.

In the Pacific, the use of fighter and bomber planes was crucial. The Japanese Zero fighter plane was a lethal aircraft, and the United States needed planes to counter it. Carrier-based aircraft were used to attack Japanese positions on islands and to provide close air support for troop landings. Through America's industrial might, more than one hundred and fifty aircraft carriers were built and launched during World War II. Damaged or destroyed carriers could be replaced at a pace the Japanese simply could not match.

Aircraft carriers changed the course of warfare forever. A single aircraft carrier group can deliver a tremendous amount of force anywhere in the world. These warships have become the point on the sword of American military might.

Gerald Ford was an unassuming and rather modest man. He was a midwesterner, and he was not prone to boasting or acting as if he were the most important person in the room. When he entered active naval service, he took on duty as an athletic officer. In addition to training future pilots in navigation, seamanship, and other skills, he drew from his background to coach various sports, including football and boxing.

The military used athletic competitions as a morale-building tool during the war. Different units would field their own football, basketball, and baseball teams. Company boxing matches were very popular. Despite the bumbling reputation he acquired later in life, Ford was likely the most athletic president to ever occupy the Oval Office.

And it was his athleticism that may have saved him as he served aboard the USS *Monterey* during the typhoon.

Winds blasted the *Monterey* with gusts of more than 100 knots (115 mph). Belowdecks, as the ship pitched in the monster waves—some more than seventy feet high—a bomber broke loose from its moorings. It rolled free and collided with the wall. The collision caused a fuel leak. When some sort of spark occurred, the fuel ignited. Aviation fuel is incredibly flammable, and within seconds a huge fire was burning. There is seldom anything sailors fear more than a fire aboard ship.

When the fire started, Lieutenant Ford was on the bridge. He was the officer of the deck: when battle stations were called, it was his job to receive information from each section of the ship and inform the captain. As news of the fire reached the bridge, the captain ordered Ford belowdecks to assess the situation. The fire caused the deaths of three sailors and injured dozens more. The ship went dead in the water. Yet the crew valiantly fought the fire, finally extinguishing it and getting under way.

On Ford's way back to the bridge, the disabled ship violently pitched in a huge wave. The wave hit the lieutenant with full force and swept him toward the edge of the deck. Ford's foot caught in a drain, which slowed his slide. He tumbled toward the edge. Onboard an aircraft carrier there is a small steel lip around the deck. Ford collided with the lip, which further slowed his fall. He tumbled over the side, but luckily the ship lurched, and he was able to twist his body and crash into the catwalk below the deck. It was a close call. As Ford later wrote in his auto-biography, "I was lucky; I could have easily gone overboard."

Ford was able to return to the bridge and report to the cap-tain. The *Monterey* survived the typhoon but was severely dam-aged. It had to leave the South Pacific and return to Bremerton, Washington, for repairs. Overall, eight hundred men were lost during the storm. Ford was discharged from the service in Feb-ruary 1946.

★ ★ ★

Ford was elected to the House of Representatives in 1963. In 1973, President Richard Nixon appointed him vice president when the sitting vice president, Spiro Agnew, resigned. Ford then assumed the presidency in 1974, when Nixon resigned in the face of the Watergate scandal. Nixon later received a full presidential pardon from Ford. It was a controversial move, and many voters did not support the decision to pardon Nixon. As an unelected president, Ford generally received lukewarm support from the American public. And, in addition to his brush with death during his military days, he also survived two assassination attempts during his time in office.

Despite his reputation for being clumsy, Gerald R. Ford knew how to duck.

IN THE BELLY OF
THE BEAST

IT WAS CALLED THE Atomic Age.

The United States dropped two atomic bombs on Japan to bring World War II to a close. The power of the atom had been harnessed to devastating effect. The postwar world ushered in an era where nuclear power was looked at as a potential energy source. Nuclear submarines and battleships were built. Nuclear reactors were planned and constructed to provide energy. Many believed the promise of nuclear power would lead the world to a scientific and social utopia.

Not so fast.

Nuclear energy is created when an atom is split. It is a dangerous process that must be carefully controlled. It creates a great amount of energy. It also causes great amounts of nuclear waste to form. This waste must be handled carefully and stored because it will not lose its radioactivity for thousands of years. There is also the potential for a nuclear reactor to fail. If this happens and a reactor overheats, its internal components can begin to melt. This is often referred to as a "meltdown." The reactor becomes superheated. Water is flooded into the reactor's nuclear core to cool it down. This water becomes radioactive. If it leaks or is released somehow, it can contaminate an area for miles around. If people or animals are exposed to this much radiation, they can become very sick or even die.

The problems and dangers of nuclear power were not as clearly understood in the beginning of the nuclear age. The United States and the Soviet Union were in a race to create as many nuclear weapons as they could.

★ ★ ★

When the Chalk River reactor in Ontario was damaged in an accident, there was no one else more familiar with reactor technology than Admiral Hyman Rickover and his sailors in the Naval Reactors Branch. Rickover sent one of his brightest men, Lieutenant James Earl Carter. Carter led the team that would fix the broken reactor.

When Carter and his team arrived in Chalk River, the first thing they did was to build an exact duplicate of the reactor on a nearby tennis court. Once the model was completed, they used it to practice the repairs they would need to make when they were in the reactor core. There was limited knowledge about the effects of radiation exposure in those days, but they knew they couldn't be in the reactor for long, so it was important to anticipate and practice exactly what to do as well as they could.

Each part of the model was labeled and numbered, and the team practiced the repair down to every last detail–in particular, they would remove as many nuts and bolts as they could as quickly as possible.

ADMIRAL HYMAN RICKOVER—FATHER OF THE NUCLEAR NAVY

He was the longest-serving naval officer and one of the longest-serving military officers in US history, with sixty-three years of service. Rickover supervised the development of nuclear-powered warships, including submarines, in the post–World War II navy. And when a nuclear reactor was near meltdown in Canada, Rickover sent Lieutenant James Earl Carter to the site with a team and instructions to "fix it." From the development stage to today's fleet, the US Navy has never suffered a nuclear accident.

Rickover graduated from the Naval Academy in 1922. After World War II, he went to work on ways to power naval vessels through nuclear power. Rickover was famous for holding officers to exacting standards. He personally interviewed every officer who served on a nuclear vessel (more than ten thousand interviews). Many officers in the navy resented Rickover. They felt his strictness kept them from receiving promotions or assignments. Yet it could be argued that his methods have kept the US Navy from a nuclear accident since the program's inception.

Then came time to enter the actual reactor. "We would dash in there as quickly as we could and take off as many bolts as we could, the same bolts we had just been practicing on," Carter recalled. "Each time our men managed to remove a bolt or fitting from the core, the equivalent piece was removed on the mock-up."

There were twenty-four men in the unit, which Carter divided into teams of three. Each team could only spend ninety seconds in the reactor core. That brief amount of time was all the human body could be exposed to at those levels. The crew absorbed more radiation in a minute and a half than a human should be exposed to in a year. The teams rotated through the reactor core, ninety seconds at a time, until the repairs were completed. "Then we went down below into the reactor room," recalled Carter. "We dashed on the site there and, in a highly radioactive environment, did our job."

The meltdown was prevented, and the reactor went on to function for decades after the accident.

The actions of Carter and his team helped prevent a meltdown that could have caused unknown damage and loss of life. For months afterward, Carter and the other men on the mission had to collect their urine and other bodily discharges, since every bit was radioactive. All of it needed to be tested until the results showed that the men could safely resume their normal lives. "I had radioactive urine for six months," Carter recalled. Just one of the side effects of when a future president decides to go crawling around inside a leaking nuclear reactor.

10

"HONEY, I FORGOT TO DUCK!"

PRESIDENT RONALD REAGAN HAD just delivered a speech to a luncheon held during a convention of the AFL-CIO labor organization at the Hilton Hotel in Washington, DC. It was a brisk, rainy spring day in the nation's capital, and in line with his reputation as a healthy, vigorous man, Reagan did not wear an overcoat.

The Hilton was a favorite venue of the Secret Service. It was much easier to secure for presidential visits, given its interior architecture. Because of that, Reagan was not wearing a bulletproof vest. Nor were any of the Secret Service agents. Their only exposure to a risk of virtually any type would be the thirty-foot walk from the hotel door to the president's waiting limousine.

Presidential security is a well-defined and calculated operation. The United States Secret Service studies, practices, and considers countless different scenarios in case of an attack on the president. Washington-based agents train at the Secret Service facility in Beltsville, Maryland, for two out of every eight weeks. Still, with a determined assassin, it is difficult if not impossible to prevent any harm from coming to the people they protect. President Lyndon Johnson once said, "All a man needs is a willingness to trade his life for mine."

Ronald Reagan's thirty-foot walk from the hotel to the limousine was the weak point in the president's security that day. For reasons unknown, a small crowd was allowed to gather behind a rope line outside the hotel entrance. This is where the assassin waited.

JOHN WARNOCK HINCKLEY JR.

It sounds like the plot to a Hollywood movie. In many ways it was. John Warnock Hinckley Jr. had become obsessed with the actress Jodie Foster, after seeing her appearance in the movie *Taxi Driver*.

Born into a wealthy Texas family, Hinckley attended Highland Park High School in Texas. There he played several sports and was even elected class president two times. After high school, Hinckley bounced around the country, randomly attending colleges and making a foray to Los Angeles in an attempt to become a songwriter. He had no success and returned to his parents' home, which was now in Colorado.

While in Colorado, something shifted for Hinckley. He purchased weapons and practiced with them. His obsession with Jodie Foster grew. When he learned she had enrolled in Yale University, Hinckley moved to New Haven, Connecticut, where the school is located. He began stalking her. He would slip notes under her door or call her on the phone.

He finally concocted a plot to do something dramatic that he believed would show his love for her. He thought of hijacking a plane, and he was arrested for attempting to carry a gun aboard a flight. Eventually, like the fictional Travis Bickle in *Taxi Driver*, he developed the idea to assassinate the president. He started following President Jimmy Carter and was arrested on gun charges in Nashville when Carter was in town, but police and FBI never made a connection.

Eventually Hinckley turned his attention to President Reagan, who was elected in 1980. His attempt to kill Reagan was nearly successful. At his trial, he was found guilty by reason of insanity and confined to a mental institution. The verdict sparked a great deal of outrage among the public and led to many changes in the insanity defense.

As President Reagan strolled toward the waiting limousine, John Hinckley fired six shots at the president in less than two seconds. One of the bullets ricocheted off the limousine and struck him beneath the arm, penetrating his chest and puncturing a lung. Other shots struck a Secret Service agent, a DC police officer, and presidential press secretary James Brady, who was gravely injured.

The Secret Service took quick action. An agent covered President Reagan with his own body and shoved him into the limo. Several citizens jumped on Hinckley, wrestling him to the ground. The remaining Secret Service agents moved in to take custody of the shooter.

Pictures of the aftermath show a Secret Service agent holding a machine gun. Many assumed this stance was to fend off another attempt. Actually, the agent was defending the shooter against a potential attack by the public. John F. Kennedy's assassin, Lee Harvey Oswald, was shot by a private citizen while in custody. Ever since then, the Secret Service has practiced and drilled for subduing, arresting, and then protecting potential assassins from harm by others or from taking their own lives. Both Theodore and Franklin Roosevelt had to command crowds to leave would-be presidential assassins to the authorities.

With President Reagan now in the back, the limousine sped toward the White House. The White House has secure, staffed, and fully stocked medical facilities. At first no one believed the president was injured. He remarked that his rib hurt and might have been broken. But then he began to cough up blood. The agents in the limo made an immediate decision to transport the president to George Washington University Hospital, which was a level-one trauma center. It was also regularly inspected by the Secret Service for safety and security in case the president needed it. There was even a dedicated phone, called "the White Phone," in the emergency room that connected directly to the White House. On this day it rang. A nurse named Wendy Koenig answered it. A voice on the other end of the line informed her: "The presidential motorcade is en route to your facility." The caller never identified himself and disconnected. A few minutes later, the phone rang again. This time a voice said, "We have three gunshot wounds coming in."

The clock was ticking now. Emergency medical personnel use a term known as "the Golden Hour": if patients receive treatment within the first hour of being injured, their chances for recovering improve dramatically. But in those days, communications were much less secure than they are today. No one mentioned to the emergency-room personnel that the president was on the way. For all the Secret Service knew at this point, President Reagan's attacker could be part of a larger plot. They kept information at a minimum when communicating through unsecured phones and radios.

The emergency room at George Washington University Hospital sprang into action. Trauma teams were assembled. Supplies were arranged and readied. When the presidential limo arrived, President Reagan insisted on walking into the hospital. Once inside he told medical personnel, "I feel like I can't catch my breath." Reagan nearly fainted, caught by his agents and a nurse, who carried him to a stretcher.

★　★　★

The president was badly injured. When his suit and other clothing were cut off, a small wound from the .22 caliber bullet was found beneath his arm. One of the Secret Service agents remarked that it looked like he was stabbed with a small knife. The president still complained of difficulty breathing.

A check of his blood pressure revealed it was very low, the sign of a patient going into shock. Shock occurs when a patient doesn't have enough blood supply to circulate throughout the body. The body begins to compensate by "pulling" all the available blood to the brain, heart, lungs, and other most-vital organs. This can cause a patient to feel cool and appear pale.

The doctors realized they would need to operate on the president. Calls went out to surgeons in the hospital to report to the ER stat. "Stat" means immediately. Doctors from all over the hospital flooded the emergency room. Even ER personnel who had gone home after their shifts answered the page and returned at once.

President Reagan continued informing the medical staff that he was having trouble breathing. Soon his wife, First Lady Nancy Reagan, arrived at his bedside. The president was famous for his sense of humor and sharp wit, even in the midst of stressful situations. He told her, "Honey, I forgot to duck!"

An X-ray revealed that the bullet had lodged near Reagan's heart. As he was wheeled into the operating room, his wit surfaced again. Looking at the doctors, he said, "Please tell me you're all Republicans!"

One of the surgeons, Dr. Joseph Giordano, who happened to be a liberal Democrat, replied, "Today we are all Republicans, Mr. President."

The operation was a tense affair. Even with an X-ray, the

surgeons had difficulty locating the bullet. They searched, but no matter where they looked, they could not find it. Finally, it was discovered in the lung tissue. It had flattened to the size and shape of a dime. Once the bullet was removed, the surgeons closed the incisions and sent Reagan to the recovery room.

From the beginning, Reagan's personal physician had insisted that the president be treated like any other patient. Throughout his stay in the hospital, he was treated like a regular seventy-year-old man. Doctors marveled at President Reagan's health and excellent physical shape. He was an active outdoorsman and loved working on his ranch in California.

During his several weeks of recovery, the hospital was turned into a miniature fortress for the president's security. Meals and medical supplies were brought from the White House, where the security could be more tightly controlled. When it was time for medication to be administered, a Secret Service agent would randomly select the medicine from the dispensary. Secure phone lines were set up. Considering the severity of his wounds, the president recovered relatively quickly.

In a strange coincidence, President Reagan attended a fund-raiser at Ford's Theatre a few weeks before he was shot. During his speech he remarked: "I looked up at the presidential box above the stage where Abe Lincoln had been sitting the night he was shot and felt a curious sensation . . . I thought that even with all the Secret Service protection we now had, it was probably still possible for someone who had enough determination to get close enough to the president to shoot him."

It was a very close call, and it required the skills and efforts of dozens of individuals to save the president's life. As could be expected, the experience had a profound effect on President

Reagan. After he had fully recovered, he spent a great deal of time pondering what had happened to him. Before entering politics, President Reagan had been an actor in Hollywood. He was a polished and eloquent speaker and was known as the "Great Communicator." After taking time to reflect on his close call, Reagan wrote in his journal: "Whatever happens now, I owe my life to God and will try to serve him in any way I can."

11

A YOUNG PILOT SAVED FROM CAPTURE

GEORGE H. W. BUSH was one of the youngest pilots in the United States Navy during World War II. He was not quite nineteen years old when he earned his wings. The future president flew multiple combat missions over the South Pacific. A decorated pilot, he won several awards and citations for bravery in combat.

And on one fateful day, he was shot down. Forced to bail out of his plane into the vast and terrifying Pacific Ocean.

And were it not for the actions of some very brave men, a fate worse than death might have awaited him.

★ ★ ★

It was a quiet Sunday morning at Naval Station Pearl Harbor, Honolulu, Hawaii, on December 7, 1941. Sailors, soldiers, and marines were just waking up to another gorgeous day in paradise.

Several hundred had already been through the mess hall for breakfast. Many had plans to return to their bunks for more sleep (what the navy called "rack time"). Church services were just beginning, and some others were only now returning to the base after a night of shore leave in downtown Honolulu.

Shortly before eight o'clock that morning, the peaceful world around them came rapidly and violently apart.

A throng of Japanese Imperial Navy aircraft plunged out of the skies above Pearl Harbor and nearby Hickam Field, where dozens of US aircraft were parked. Like a swarm of angry wasps, the airplanes wreaked havoc on the fleet of ships, aircraft, and facilities. Explosion after explosion shattered the morning calm, and the resulting chaos left thousands of military and civilian personnel dead and wounded.

The Japanese targeted the American battleships. It was easy to do, since almost all of them were in port and docked on Battleship Row in the harbor. Confusion reigned at first. Military members and civilians alike did not understand or believe that an attack was under way. For the Japanese pilots it was what is known as a target-rich environment. The Japanese used over three hundred and fifty aircraft in two waves of attacks and inflicted tremendous damage on the US fleet. Several ships, including the battleship USS *Arizona*, were sunk. Virtually every aircraft on the ground was destroyed or damaged in the attack. The only saving grace for the United States was that none of the fleet's aircraft carriers were docked at Pearl Harbor during the attack. They were all at sea taking part in battle simulations. The US submarine force was also spread out in various locations and spared damage in the initial onslaught.

The news of the attack stunned America. The next day, President Roosevelt addressed a joint session of Congress and asked for a declaration of war against Imperial Japan and Nazi Germany. The United States was now directly involved in a war much of the world was already fighting. The Japanese decision to attack Pearl Harbor sealed our fate as a world power. Though they delivered a crippling blow, they could not defeat the United States, with its seemingly endless supply of manpower and industrial might. The commander of the Japanese fleet, Admiral Yamamoto, made a profound observation after the attack on Pearl Harbor. He said, "I fear all we have done is awaken a sleeping giant and fill him with a terrible resolve."

★ ★ ★

On his eighteenth birthday, June 12, 1942, George Herbert Walker Bush enlisted in the US Navy. Like many men of his generation, he decided to join up right away, rather than wait to be drafted. He reported for active duty in August of that year. He enrolled in flight training at the University of North Carolina at Chapel Hill. It was a ten-month course, and he earned his wings.

The young Ensign Bush spent time in the United States on assignment as a flight instructor. Then he was ordered to report to the USS *San Jacinto*, an aircraft carrier operating in the South Pacific. Bush had been promoted to lieutenant and was now piloting the TBF Avenger. The Avenger was a plane specially developed for the navy and designed to deliver either torpedo bombs or traditional ordnance. The Avenger was a powerful airplane with a three-man crew, including a gunner and a navigator/bombardier.

In September 1944 Lieutenant Bush was on a mission to the Chichi Jima islands, a heavily fortified Japanese installation with a tremendous amount of antiaircraft artillery deployed across the island. His orders were to bomb military targets, including a large radio tower. Lieutenant Bush's plane was one of four Avengers that were ordered to begin a bombing run over the island. All of the planes were hit, including the one piloted by the forty-first president. But Lieutenant Bush managed to steer his plane out to sea.

The plane was on fire, and the cockpit filled with smoke. Bush stayed at the controls and ordered his crewmates to bail out. He steered the Avenger into a banked turn to make it easier for his crew to escape. Tragedy struck, however, when one of his crew was killed by gunfire and another's parachute failed to open before he plunged into the sea.

Bush kept his aircraft aloft as long as he could. When he was several miles away from the island, he finally had to bail out. "It was when I saw the flame along the wing there that I said, 'I better get out of here,'" he recalled during the interview. "I dove out onto the wing. I hit my head on the tail, a glancing blow, and was bleeding like a stuck pig."

Amazingly, Bush survived. "I dropped into the ocean, and I swam over and got into this life raft," he remembered. "I was sick to my stomach. I was scared." Other American planes circled above him. But he was not out of danger yet.

A former squadron mate of Bush's, Charlie Bynum, recalled, "We saw him in the water. And we saw the Japanese boats coming out from land to pick him up. They had guns on him."

The first boat approached. Bush was alone in the small raft, with no weapon or means to defend himself.

The boat drew closer.

Gunfire sounded, and the boat veered away. Bush looked up to see a US Navy plane, flown by Lieutenant Doug West, strafing the boat with its machine guns.

Other aircraft in the area continued circling as Bush floated in the raft, protecting him from his potential captors.

Another boat zoomed out from the island.

An F4 Wildcat flown by a navy pilot fired his guns and the boat steered away.

Lieutenant Bush understood that it might be hours or even days until he could be rescued by a ship or submarine. All he could do was hope the navy pilots would be able to fend off the Japanese. As well as he could, Bush paddled the small raft, trying to get as far away from Chichi Jima island as possible.

Another boat made a run at the raft only to be driven back by another navy pilot. Bush waved at the airplane and the pilot dipped his wings, letting the young lieutenant know that he was not going to be abandoned.

At this point in the war, the United States military knew how brutal and inhumane captivity was for Japanese prisoners of war. The Japanese empire practiced a form of extreme nationalism. Nationalism is a belief that a nation and its citizens are superior to all other nations, and therefore people are not required to conform to the standards set by other countries. During the decades before World War II, Japan refused to sign the Geneva conventions, a series of treaties between nations that governed (among other things) how prisoners were to be treated in wartime.

Prisoners were horribly treated in camps all over the Pacific theater during the war. They were given little food and virtually no medical care. The Japanese also refused to allow organizations like the Red Cross to deliver any food or medical supplies to prisoners. Torture and abuse were common. Prisoners were often beaten and executed.

Pilots were especially hated by the Japanese, and American pilots would do almost anything to avoid being captured. While Lieutenant Bush floated in the open sea, his fellow flyers were determined to save him from capture if they could. But they would not be able to stay in the air above him forever. They did not carry enough fuel, and replacement aircraft couldn't reach the site from the USS *San Jacinto* in time.

The first hour went by. Planes continued to circle above him. Each time a Japanese boat approached, a navy pilot would drive it back. Bush spent the next three hours bobbing in the waves, bleeding and seasick, using what little strength he had left to try and paddle away from the island. Pilots who spent time in the Pacific would often talk about the vastness of the ocean. Young Lieutenant Bush must have felt very small in his tiny raft as he awaited his fate.

Finally, after nearly four hours in the raft, Bush spotted a periscope in the water a few yards away from his raft. All he could do was hope that there wasn't a Japanese submarine below. But luck was still with young Bush that day. The USS *Finback* surfaced and pulled the pilot aboard. Later he recalled, "I saw this thing coming out of the water, and I said to myself, 'Jeez, I hope it's one of ours.'" Bush was injured, still bleeding from his head wound. He continued to vomit from swallowing seawater in his desperate swim away from Chichi Jima. But he still greeted his rescuers with, "Happy to be here."

★ ★ ★

Lieutenant Bush spent a month aboard the USS *Finback*. He found the experience claustrophobic, particularly when the sub was being assaulted by depth charges.

"I thought being rescued by the submarine was the end of my problem. I didn't realize that I would have to spend the duration of the sub's thirty remaining days on board."

WORLD WAR II SUBMARINE WARFARE IN THE PACIFIC

"Execute unrestricted air and submarine warfare against Japan."
—Order issued by Admiral H. R. Stark, the Chief of Naval Operations in Washington, following the Japanese attack on Pearl Harbor, Hawaii, on December 7, 1941.

When the Japanese attacked Pearl Harbor, the United States Navy had about fifty serviceable submarines deployed in the Pacific theater. With the fleet's battleships nearly crippled, the submarine force assumed a central role in taking the fight to the enemy. By the time the war ended, submarines had sunk over 30 percent of Japan's navy.

A little-known fact about World War II–era submarines is that they were mostly surface ships that could only travel underwater for a limited time. When submerged they ran on electric motors powered by batteries. The batteries could only be recharged when the submarine surfaced. Once on the surface they used diesel engines and could travel at a much faster rate of speed. Because they had the ability to travel for weeks without being resupplied or refueled, it gave them a prominent role in isolating the island of Japan. With submarines sinking Japanese merchant ships, the country's economy and war machine was crippled.

By the end of the war, the US Navy deployed nearly three hundred submarines in the Pacific theater alone. Their versatility in combat operations, from offensive campaigns to search and rescue, ushered in a new type of warfare. In the years after World War II, submarines became nuclear powered, larger, and capable of longer deployments. The submarine became a sophisticated and potent weapon in America's military strategy.

"I thought I was scared at times flying into combat, but in a submarine, you couldn't do anything except sit there. The submariners were saying that it must be scary to be shot at by anti-aircraft fire and I was saying to myself, 'Listen, brother, it is not really as bad as what you go through.'"

While on the USS *Finback*, future President Bush recounted how he often thought of the men he flew with and his own crew, who perished in the fight. "Why had I been spared? . . . In my own view there's got to be some kind of destiny, and I was being spared for something on Earth."

SOURCES

★ George Washington ★

QUOTATIONS

p. 3: "The greatest and vilest attempt": Gary Shattuck, "Plotting the 'Sacricide' of George Washington," *Journal of the American Revolution*, https://allthingsliberty.com/2014/07/plotting-the-sacricide-of-george -washington/, accessed July 15, 2015.

p. 4: " prevent any future correspondence": George Washington to New York Committee of Safety, April 17, 1776, in *Founders Online* (National Archives), https://founders.archives.gov/documents /Washington/03-04-02-0061, accessed July 15, 2015.

p. 4: "The encouragements given": George Washington to John Hancock, June 10, 1776, in *Founders Online* (National Archives), https://founders .archives.gov/documents/Washington/03-04-02-0382, accessed July 15, 2015.

p. 6: "a plot as has seldom appeared . . . rise against the country": Gary Shattuck, "Plotting the 'Sacricide' of George Washington."

p. 9: "Before another day": Patti Wigington, "Thinker, Tailor, Soldier, Spy: Who Was the Real Hercules Mulligan?" ThoughtCo, https://www .thoughtco.com/hercules-mulligan-4160489, accessed July 14, 2019.

ADDITIONAL SOURCES

American Battlefield Trust. "Clothier to General Washington and Patriot Spy: Hercules Mulligan." https://www.battlefields.org/learn/articles/hercules -mulligan, accessed July 14, 2019.

Central Intelligence Agency. "The Legend of Hercules Mulligan." https:// www.cia.gov/news-information/featured-story-archive/2016-featured-story -archive/the-legend-of-hercules-mulligan.html, accessed July 14, 2019.

Chernow, Ron. *Alexander Hamilton*. New York: Random House, 2005.

McBurney, Christian. "The Plot to Kidnap Washington." *Military History Quarterly*. August 15, 2017.

Nagy, John. *George Washington's Secret Spy War: The Making of America's First Spymaster*. New York: St. Martin's Press, 2017.

Rose, Alexander. *Washington's Spies: The Story of America's First Spy Ring*. New York: Bantam Books, 2007.

★ Andrew Jackson ★

SELECTED SOURCES

Boissoneault, Lorraine. "The Attempted Assassination of Andrew Jackson." *Smithsonian Magazine*. https://www.smithsonianmag.com/history /attempted-assassination-andrew-jackson-180962526/, accessed July 14, 2019.

Medved, Michael. *The American Miracle: Divine Providence in the Rise of the Republic*. New York: Crown Forum, 2016.

National Park Services. "Andrew Jackson Gains his Nicknames." https://www .nps.gov/natr/learn/historyculture/andrew-jackson-gains-his-nicknames. html, accessed July 14, 2019.

★ Abraham Lincoln ★

QUOTATIONS

p. 22: "I shall do all that may be in my power": Abraham Lincoln, "Address to the New Jersey State Senate," speech, Trenton, New Jersey, February 21, 1861, Abraham Lincoln Online, http://www.abrahamlincolnonline.org /lincoln/speeches/trenton1.htm, accessed July 15, 2015.

p. 26: "I cannot go tonight": Daniel Stashower, "The Unsuccessful Plot to Kill Abraham Lincoln," *Smithsonian Magazine*, February 2013, https:// www.smithsonianmag.com/history/the-unsuccessful-plot-to-kill-abraham -lincoln-2013956/, accessed July 14, 2019.

p. 32: "It's to be hoped": Walter Coffey, The Civil War Months, "Lincoln Sneaks Into Washington," https://civilwarmonths.com/2016/02/22/lincoln -sneaks-into-washington/, accessed July 14, 2019.

p. 32: "I had informed": Daniel Stashower, "The Unsuccessful Plot to Kill Abraham Lincoln."

ADDITIONAL SOURCES

Goodwin, Doris Kearns. *Team of Rivals: The Political Genius of Abraham Lincoln*. New York: Simon and Schuster, 2005.

Holzer, Harold. "Lincoln's Tough Guy: Ward Hill Lamon." *Civil War Times*. February 22, 2017.

Pinkerton, Allan. *The Spy of the Rebellion; Being a True History of the Spy System of the United States Army During the Late Rebellion.* NP: 1883. Project Guttenberg, 2011: https://www.gutenberg.org/files/34973/34973 -h/34973-h.htm, accessed July 14, 2019.

Stashower, Daniel. *The Hour of Peril: The Secret Plot to Murder Lincoln Before the Civil War.* New York: Minotaur, 2013.

★ Theodore Roosevelt ★

QUOTATIONS

p. 35: "I don't know whether you fully understand. . . . to kill a Bull Moose": Theodore Roosevelt Center, "It Takes More Than That to Kill a Bull Moose," https://www.theodorerooseveltcenter.org/Blog/Item/It%20takes%20more%20 than%20that%20to%20kill%20a%20Bull%20Moose, accessed July 14, 2019.

p. 38: "Don't hurt him. . . . to the police": Christopher Klein, "When Teddy Roosevelt Was Shot in 1912, a Speech May Have Saved His Life," History Stories, the History Channel, October 12, 2012, https://www.history.com /news/shot-in-the-chest-100-years-ago-teddy-roosevelt-kept-on-talking, accessed July 14, 2019.

p. 39: "Now, friends": Theodore Roosevelt Center, "It Takes More Than That to Kill a Bull Moose."

ADDITIONAL SOURCES

Helfrich, Gerald. *Theodore Roosevelt and the Assassin: Madness, Vengeance, and the Campaign of 1912.* Guilford, CT: Lyons Press, 2013.

National Parks Service. "Who Shot T.R.?" https://www.nps.gov/thrb/learn /historyculture/whoshottr.htm, accessed July 14, 2019.

O'Toole, Patricia. "The Speech that Saved Teddy Roosevelt's Life." *Smithsonian Magazine.* https://www.smithsonianmag.com/history/the -speech-that-saved-teddy-roosevelts-life-83479091/, accessed July 14, 2019.

★ Harry S. Truman ★

SELECTED SOURCES

History.com. "An Assassination Attempt Threatens President Harry S. Truman." https://www.history.com/this-day-in-history/an-assassination- attempt-threatens-president-harry-s-truman, accessed October 29, 2019.

Mahan, Sydney. "66 Years Ago Today, President Truman Survived an Assassination Attempt at Blair House." https://www.washingtonian .com/2016/11/01/president-truman-assassination-attempt-blair-house/, accessed October 29, 2019.

McCullough, David. *Truman*, New York: Simon & Schuster, 1993.

Truman, Margaret, ed. *Where the Buck Stops: The Personal and Private Writings of Harry S. Truman*, New York: Grand Central, 1989.

★ Dwight D. Eisenhower ★

QUOTATIONS

p. 56: "Three times I was ordered to prove": Omar Bradley, "The German Hits Back," *Life Magazine,* April 23, 1951.

p. 57: "I shall not" : Smith, Stuart, *Otto Skorzeny: The Devil's Disciple,* Oxford, UK: Osprey Publishing, 2018.

ADDITIONAL SOURCES

Skorzeny, Otto. *Hitler's Commando: The Daring Missions of Otto Skorzeny and the Nazi Special Forces*. New York: Skyhorse Publishing, 2016.

Taylor, Blaine. "Intelligence: Operation Greif: Nazi Germany's Trojan Horse." International Historic Films. https://ihffilm.com/operation-greif-nazi -germany-trojan-horse-essay-by-blaine-taylor.html, accessed July 14, 2019.

Whiting, Charles. "Operation Greif: Assassinate Eisenhower." Warfare History Network. https://warfarehistorynetwork.com/daily/wwii/operation-greif -assassinate-eisenhower-2/, accessed July 14, 2019.

★ John F. Kennedy ★

QUOTATIONS

pp. 60, 63, 68, and 69: "Ship at two o'clock," "Who's aboard?," "I have a letter," and "It was involuntary": Hersey, John, "Survival," *The New Yorker*, June 17, 1944.

ADDITIONAL SOURCES

HistoryNet. "John F. Kennedy." https://www.historynet.com/john-f-kennedy, accessed July 14, 2019.

National Park Service. "John F. Kennedy: World War II Naval Hero to President."
   https://www.nps.gov/articles/kennedyww2.htm, accessed July 14, 2019.

★ Gerald Ford ★

QUOTATIONS

p. 76: "I was lucky": Gerald Ford. *A Time to Heal*. New York: HarperCollins, 1979.

ADDITIONAL SOURCES

Gerald R. Ford Museum and Library. "Naval Service of Gerald R. Ford in
   WWII." https://www.fordlibrarymuseum.gov/grf/naval.htm, accessed July
   14, 2019.
Kruzel, John J. "Authors Remember Ford's Courage During Fire in WWII."
   U.S. Department of Defense. DoD News. https://archive.defense.gov
   /news/NewsArticle.aspx?ID=2574, accessed October 12, 2019.

★ Jimmy Carter ★

QUOTATIONS

p. 82: "We would dash in there. . . . on the mock-up," "Then we went down…
   did our job," and "I had radioactive urine": Carter, Jimmy, *A Full Life:
   Reflections at Ninety*, New York: Simon & Schuster, 2016.

ADDITIONAL SOURCES

Milnes, Arthur. "Jimmy Carter's Exposure to Nuclear Danger." April 5, 2011.
   http://www.cnn.com/2011/OPINION/04/05/milnes.carter.nuclear/index
   .html, accessed August 6, 2019.

★ Ronald Reagan ★

QUOTATIONS

pp. 86, 89, and 90: "All a man needs," "The presidential motorcade,"
   "Please tell me," and "Today we are all": John Pekkanen, "The Saving
   of the President," *Washingtonian*, March 20, 2011, https://www

.washingtonian.com/2011/03/10/the-saving-of-the-president/, accessed July 15, 2019.

pp. 91 and 92: "I looked up at the presidential box" and "any way I can": Del Quentin Wilber, *Rawhide Down: The Near Assassination of Ronald Reagan*, New York: Picador, 2012.

ADDITIONAL SOURCES

Brands, H. W. *Reagan: The Life*. New York: Random House, 2015
Silverleib, Alan. "The Day That Changed Presidential Security Forever." CNN. March 30, 2011. http://www.cnn.com/2011/POLITICS/03/30/hinckley.presidential.protection/index.html, accessed July 15, 2019.

★ George H. W. Bush ★

QUOTATIONS

p. 97: "I fear all we have done": "Why the Man who Planned the Attacks on Pearl Harbor Advised Against Them," Pearl Harbor Visitors Bureau, https://visitpearlharbor.org/man-who-planned-the-attacks/, accessed August 6, 2019.

p. 98: "It was when" and "I dropped into the ocean": Richard Sisk, "'Fair Winds and Following Seas, Mr. President,' Former Pres. Bush Remembered," Military.com, December 1, 2018. https://www.military.com/daily-news/2018/12/01/fair-winds-and-following-seas-mr-president-former-president-bush-remembered.html, accessed August 6, 2019.

p. 98: "We saw him in the water": "Story of George H. W. Bush World War II Experience," *CNN Presents*, December 20, 2003 (transcript), http://transcripts.cnn.com/TRANSCRIPTS/0312/20/cp.00.html, accessed August 6, 2019.

p. 100: "I saw this thing": "George H. W. Bush: The War Years," BBC News, December 1, 2018, https://www.bbc.com/news/world-us-canada-12925591, accessed August 6, 2019.

p. 101: "I thought being rescued": James Bradley, *Flyboys: A True Story of Courage*, New York: Little, Brown and Company, 2003.

ADDITIONAL SOURCES

Jones, Matthew. "Before He Was President, George H. W. Bush Was a Pilot." *The Virginian-Pilot*. January 9, 2009. https://pilotonline.com/news/military /article_33cedfb9-e653-5cd0-84a1-1ebf56115254.html, accessed July 15, 2019.

INDEX

Adams, John Quincy, 16–17
African Americans
  Cato's role during Revolution,
    7, 9–10
  Eisenhower's policy toward, 52
  World War II plot foiled by, 52,
    54–57
Agnew, Spiro, 76
Aircraft carriers
  Bush (George H. W.) service
    on, 97
  Ford's survival during typhoon
    and fire, 72–76
  role in World War II, 73–74
  spared in Pearl Harbor attack,
    96
Amagiri (Japanese destroyer),
  60–65
American Revolution, 1–11
  British loyalists (Tories) in,
    4–7
  British spying in, 4–11
  foiling plots during (Mulligan
    and Cato), 7–11
  Hickey plot in, 2–7
  military tactics in, 2
Atomic Age, 79–80
Atomic bomb, 44–45, 79
Avenger airplane, 97–98

Baltimore plot, against Lincoln,
  21–32
Battle of the Bulge, German plot
  during, 52–57
Birdzell, Donald, 47

Blackett Strait, 64
Bradley, Omar, 56–57
Brady, James, 88
"The buck stops here" (Truman
  saying), 45
Bull Moose Party, 35, 37–39
Bush, George H. W.
  air efforts to protect, 99–100
  plane shot down, 97–103
  potential fate as prisoner,
    99–100
  submarine rescue of, 100–103
  thoughts on destiny, 103
  wartime service of, x, 95, 97

Carter, Jimmy
  exposure to radioactivity, 83
  role in preventing nuclear
    meltdown, 80–83
  sentence commuted by, 48
Cato (slave and spy), 7, 9–10
Chalk River reactor (Ontario),
  80–83
Chichi Jima island, 98–100
Churchill, Winston, 45
Civil War
  Baltimore plot against Lincoln,
    21–32
  secession of Southern states,
    21–22
Clarke, Bruce, 55
Clay, Henry, 17
Coffelt, Leslie, 47
Collazo, Oscar, 46–48
Committee of Safety, 4–6

"Corrupt Bargain" (1824 election),
  16–17
Crockett, Davy, 14–15, 18
Culper Ring, 10

Davies, Henry, 24
Davis, Warren, 15
Declaration of Independence,
  1–2
Detectives
  first woman detective in U.S.,
    26–29
  Pinkerton and Lincoln
    protection, 23–32
"Devil boats," PT boats as,
  61–62
Doolittle, Jimmy, 73

Eisenhower, Dwight D.
  German spying and plot
    against, 51–57
  integration efforts of, 52
  as Supreme Commander,
    51–52
Espionage. See Spies

The Federalist Papers, 8
Ferguson Passage, 64–65
Ford, Gerald, 71–76
  aircraft carrier typhoon and
    fire, 72–76
  ascension to presidency, 76
  assassination attempts against,
    76
  athleticism of, 71–72, 74–75
  modesty of, 74
  reputation for being clumsy,
    71, 76
Foster, Jodie, 86–87

Geneva conventions, 99
George III (king of Great Britain),
  1–2
George Washington University
  Hospital, 88–92
Germany, spies and plots in World
  War II, 51–57
Giordano, Joseph, 90
"Golden Hour," in medical care,
  89
Great Britain
  Americans loyal to (Tories), 4–7
  plots against Washington,
    2–11
  revolt against, 1–2
  spying during American
    Revolution, 4–11
Great Communicator, Reagan as,
  92

Halsey, William "Bull," 72–73
Hamilton, Alexander, 8–10
Hickey, Thomas, 2, 7
Hickey plot, 2–7
Hinckley, John W., Jr., 86–88
Hitler, Adolf, 53
"Hooligan Navy," PT boats in, 62
Howe, William, 10

Indian Removal Act, 14–15

Jackson, Andrew, 13–19
  attempted assassination of, x,
    15–19
  Crockett and, 14–15, 18
  loss in "Corrupt Bargain,"
    16–17
  Old Hickory nickname of, 16,
    19

prospective assassin's anger
toward, 18–19
shooter beaten by, 16–18
Japan
attack on Pearl Harbor, 95–97,
101
Bush (George H. W.) shot
down by, 97–103
sinking of PT-109, 59–69
treatment of prisoners of war,
99–100
Johnson, Lyndon, 86

Kennedy, John F.
assassination of, 88
coconut shell message of,
66–67
health and military discharge
of, 68
mourning of lost crew
members, 68–69
near drowning from capsized
canoe, 67
presumed death and memorial
service for, 65
PT-109 heroism and survival,
59–69
publicity, song, and movie
about war experience,
68–69
rescue on Nauru, 66–68
Koenig, Wendy, 89
Kolombangara Island, 60

Lamon, Ward Hill, 26, 29–31
Lawrence, Charles W. (alias of
German spy), 55
Lawrence, Richard, 15–19
Letter bomb, for Truman, 43

Lincoln, Abraham
Baltimore plot against, 21–32
disguise of, 29
as greatest president, 21
hatred toward, 21, 24
passage through Baltimore,
30–32
Pinkerton protection of,
23–32
Reagan's reference to, 91
ridicule over arrival in
Washington, 32
Southern response to election,
21–22
train schedule of, 22
warnings and pleas to, 24–28
Lincoln, Mary Todd, 26–27

McKinley, William, 38, 40–41
McMahon, Patrick "Pop," 63,
65
Meltdown, nuclear
Carter's role in preventing,
80–83
definition of, 80
Montgomery, Bernard, 55
Mulligan, Hercules, 7–11
Mulligan, Hugh, 10
Mussolini, Benito, 53

National Progressive (Bull Moose)
Party, 35, 37–39
Nationalism, 99
Nauro. See Nauru
Nauru
coconut shell message sent
from, 66–67
rescue of PT-109 survivors on,
66–68

New York City
  British spies operating in,
    4–11
  Washington's base of operations
    in, 3–4
Nixon, Richard, 76
Nuclear energy, 79–82
  Carter's role in preventing
    meltdown, 80–83
  Rickover and nuclear navy,
    80–82
  waste from, 79–80
Nuclear-powered submarines,
  102

Operation Greif (Operation Grip),
  54–57
Oswald, Lee Harvey, 88

Patrol torpedo (PT) boats, 61–62.
  See also PT-109
Pearl Harbor, 95–97, 101
Personality traits, of presidents,
  ix–x
Pinkerton, Allan, 23–32
Pinkerton National Detective
  Agency, 23, 25, 30
Plum Pudding Island, 63–65
Poison
  German cigarette lighters,
    55–56
  peas for Washington, 2–3
President(s). See also specific
  presidents
  first to survive assassination
    attempt, x, 15
  greatest, Lincoln as, 21
  personality traits of, ix–x
  power of, ix

security of, planning and
    training for, 85–86
  wartime (military) experience
    of, ix
Prisoners of war, 99–100
Propaganda, 51
PT-109
  Kennedy's coconut shell
    message, 66–67
  Kennedy's heroism and
    survival, 59–69
  Kennedy's mourning of lost
    crew members, 68–69
  mission of, 60
  as patrol torpedo boat, 61–62
  presumed death and memorial
    service for men of, 65
  publicity, song, and movie
    about, 68–69
  rescue of survivors on Nauru,
    66–68
  sinking of, 60–63
Puerto Rican Nationalist Party
  (PRNP), 46–48

Reagan, Nancy, 90
Reagan, Ronald
  as Great Communicator, 92
  humor and wit of, 90
  injuries of, 90
  motivation of shooter,
    86–87
  recovery of, 91
  reference to Lincoln, 91
  shooting of, 85–92
  shooting's impact on, 91–92
  surgery on, 90–91
  transport to hospital, 88–89
Rickover, Hyman, 80–82

Roosevelt, Franklin Delano,
43–44, 88
Roosevelt, Theodore (Teddy),
35–41, 88
Bull Moose candidacy of, 35,
37–39
bullet lodged in chest of, 39
insanity of prospective assassin,
40–41
popularity of, 36
speech delivered despite
wound, 35–36, 39–40
"strenuous life" of, 36–37
Ross, George, 64–68

Salomon, Haym, 9–10
Schrank, John Flammang, 38–41
Secession, of Southern states,
21–22
Secret Service
attempt on Truman's life and,
46–48
handling of potential assassins,
88
Johnson on qualification for,
86
legislation increasing protection
duties of, 48
Pinkerton and forerunner of,
25–26
shooting of Reagan and, 85–89
training and planning of,
85–86
Sensenbach, George (alias of
German spy), 55
Seward, Frederick, 24–28
Seward, William, 24
Shootings and shooting attempts
Jackson, 15–19

Reagan, 85–92
Roosevelt (Theodore),
35–41
Truman, 43, 46–48
Skorzeny, Otto, 53–57
Solomon Islands, PT-109 ordeal
in, 59–69
Sons of Liberty, 8–10
Spies
British, against Washington,
4–11
Culper Ring, 10
execution of, 53
German, in World War II,
51–57
Mulligan and Cato, 7–11
Pinkerton protection of
Lincoln, 23–32
Stalin, Joseph, 45
Stark, H. R., 101
"Stat," 90
"Strenuous life," of Roosevelt
(Theodore), 36–37
Submarines
nuclear-powered, 102
rescue of Bush (George H. W.),
100–103
role in World War II,
101–102
spared in Pearl Harbor attack,
96

Taft, William Howard, 37
Taxi Driver (movie), 86–87
Tories, 4–7
Torpedoes, in World War II,
61–62
Torresola, Griselo, 46–48
Truman, Bess, 47

Truman, Harry S., 43–48
  ascension to presidency,
    43–44
  "the buck stops here," 45
  decision to drop atomic bomb,
    44–45
  fondness for naps, 47
  gun battle in attempted
    assassination of, 43, 46–48
  letter bomb directed at, 43
  narrow escape of, 48
Typhoon, Ford's survival during,
  72–76
Tyron, William, 4–6

Underground Railroad, 25
USS *Finback* (submarine),
  100–103
USS *Jacinto* (aircraft carrier), 97,
  100
USS *Langley* (aircraft carrier),
  73–74
USS *Monterey* (aircraft carrier),
  72, 75–76

Van Buren, Martin, 18
van der Werth, Clarence (alias of
  German spy), 55

Warne, Kate, 26–29
Washington, George, 1–11
  British spies targeting, 4–11
  foiling plots against (Mulligan
    and Cato), 7–11
  Hickey plot against, 2–7
  military experience of, x

New York City as base of
    operations, 3–4
  support for Mulligan, 10–11
West, Doug, 99
"White Phone," at hospital, 89
Wilson, Woodrow, 37
Wincote, Lieutenant, 68
World War II
  atomic bomb in, 44–45, 79
  Bush (George H.W.) service in,
    x, 95, 97
  Bush (George H.W.) shot down
    and rescued in, 97–103
  carrier power in, 73–74
  Eisenhower as Supreme
    Commander in, 51–52
  Ford's survival in typhoon and
    fire, 72–76
  German spies and plots in,
    51–57
  Halsey's naval tactics in, 72–73
  Japanese treatment of prisoners
    in, 99–100
  Kennedy's PT-109 heroism and
    survival in, 59–69
  passwords and checkpoints in,
    55, 56–57
  patrol torpedo (PT) boats in,
    61–62
  Pearl Harbor attack in, 95–97,
    101
  propaganda in, 51
  submarines in, 101–102
  Truman's leadership in, 43–45

Yamamoto, Isoroku, 97